THE FRANCIS E. CLARK YEAR - BOOK

A Collection Of Living Paragraphs
From Addresses, Books, And
Magazine Articles By The Founder
of the
Young People's Society of Christian
Endeavor

Selected And Arranged By
John R. Clements

Introduction By Fanny J. Crosby
(The Blind Hymn - Writer)

First Fruits Press
Wilmore, Kentucky
c2015

The Francis E. Clark year-book, selected and arranged by John R. Clements, introduction by
Fanny J. Crosby.

First Fruits Press, ©2015
Previously published: Boston, Chicago: United Society of Christian Endeavor ©1904.

ISBN: 9781621713531 (print), 9781621713548 (digital)

Digital version at http://place.asburyseminary.edu/christianendeavorbooks/32/

First Fruits Press is a digital imprint of the Asbury Theological Seminary, B.L. Fisher Library.
Asbury Theological Seminary is the legal owner of the material previously published by the
Pentecostal Publishing Co. and reserves the right to release new editions of this material as well as
new material produced by Asbury Theological Seminary. Its publications are available for
noncommercial and educational uses, such as research, teaching and private study. First Fruits
Press has licensed the digital version of this work under the Creative Commons Attribution
Noncommercial 3.0 United States License. To view a copy of this license, visit
http://creativecommons.org/licenses/by-nc/3.0/us/.

For all other uses, contact:

First Fruits Press
B.L. Fisher Library
Asbury Theological Seminary
204 N. Lexington Ave.
Wilmore, KY 40390
http://place.asburyseminary.edu/firstfruits

Clark, Francis E. (Francis Edward), 1851-1927.
    The Francis E. Clark year-book / selected and arranged by John R. Clements; introduction by
Fanny J. Crosby.
    133 pages; 21 cm.
    Wilmore, Ky. : First Fruits Press, ©2015.
    Reprint. Previously published: Boston: United Society of Christian Endeavor ©1904.
    "A collection of living paragraphs from addresses, books, and magazine articles by the
    founder of the Young People's Society of Christian Endeavor."
    ISBN: 9781621713531 (pbk.)
1. Theology. I. Title. II. Clements, John R. (John Ralston), 1868-
BR85 .C52 2015

Cover design by Jonathan Ramsay

First Fruits Press

The Academic Open Press of Asbury Theological Seminary

204 N. Lexington Ave., Wilmore, KY 40390

859-858-2236

first.fruits@asburyseminary.edu

asbury.to/firstfruits

REV. F. E. CLARK, D. D.

THE

FRANCIS E. CLARK YEAR-BOOK

A COLLECTION OF LIVING PARAGRAPHS
FROM ADDRESSES, BOOKS, AND
MAGAZINE ARTICLES
BY THE FOUNDER
OF THE

YOUNG PEOPLE'S
SOCIETY OF CHRISTIAN ENDEAVOR

SELECTED AND ARRANGED BY
JOHN R. CLEMENTS

INTRODUCTION BY FANNY J. CROSBY
(*The Blind Hymn-Writer*)

United Society of Christian Endeavor
BOSTON AND CHICAGO

NOTE.—For permission to use copyright
material, hearty thanks are extended to Funk
and Wagnalls Company, Fleming H. Revell
Company, and The Christian Endeavor World

PREFACE

It is hoped that the presentation in this form of these gems, gathered from the books, magazines, articles, and convention addresses of the honored founder of the Christian Endeavor movement, may find a hearty reception and a large use.

Such a book as this is always helpful. Its message may be made ours at the opening of each day, or it may serve as an aid to our part-taking in the Christian Endeavor meeting. As a pocket companion it may give us food for reflection on many an occasion when the moments would drag heavily.

The preparation of the book has been a delight and an inspiration. It is sent on its way with the prayer that these utterances of a beloved leader may be given a new life and a larger usefulness in this form.

The proceeds from the sale of this book, so far as the compiler is concerned, shall be used for the spread of Christian Endeavor "in lands afar."

JOHN R. CLEMENTS.

"The Den," April, 1904.

A Christian Endeavor Prayer for Every Morning

Our Father in heaven, bless us who unite in this prayer to thee, and our Christian Endeavor brothers and sisters in every land.

Enlarge our fellowship; increase our faithfulness; make us more useful in thy church. Move our hearts, not only to pray, but to give as thou hast prospered us, for this and every good cause. Bring young people who know thee not to thyself. Bless, we pray thee, the Juniors, that the boys and girls may be thine.

For the Christian Endeavor brotherhood in all denominations and in all the world we thank thee. Make us worthy of large blessings, and able to receive them. For the sake of Jesus Christ, our only Lord and Saviour. Amen.

INTRODUCTION

A pleasant task is fulfilled, and lo! a little volume rich in its prolific stores comes forth to reward our hopes, and realize our anticipations. Love is its key-note and love the predominant principle in the hearts of those who were instrumental in its preparation and arrangement.

Every word which it contains is like a jewel of inestimable worth, and every page like the placid waters of a silver stream bursting from a hidden spring in a towering rock, and sparkling amid the unclouded splendor of the midday sun. In its object this little book is as pure and unselfish as the character it represents, and from whom originated the bright, pithy, and unique sayings, caught as they fell from the lips that uttered them, and transmitted without the slightest change in their construction, to beautify and adorn the pages that will yet be hailed with acclamations of joy by every Christian Endeavorer.

This work is intended as an expression of our esteem, veneration, and loyal affection for one whose entire life has been devoted to the cause and kingdom of our Lord and Master, and to the welfare of immortal souls,—one whom we sometimes designate by the endearing name of "Father Clark."

No language can portray his tender solicitude for his adopted children. He is not only the founder of our Society, but from an earthly standpoint he is our watchword and guiding star, leading us surely and steadily nearer to the great Author of our being, and to the source from whence cometh every good and perfect gift. It is not wrong to assert that in the spirit world there are thousands that owe their conversion to his influence and prayers. Even now as we write, he is abroad, bearing the gospel banner, telling the wondrous story of the cross, and proclaiming the message of redemption to the souls that are perishing.

TO OUR BELOVED

FRIEND AND SPIRITUAL GUIDE

Rev. FRANCIS E. CLARK, D.D.

the following lines are most cordially and sincerely dedicated.

> Faithful teacher, we are learning
> How the Christian race to run;
> Learning by thine own example,
> And the victories thou hast won.

There's a crown of stars that waits thee
   In the palace of the King,
And a song of grace and glory
   That forever thou wilt sing.
For the King himself will lead thee
   To the banquet of his love,
And present thee pure and spotless
   At his Father's throne above.

FANNY J. CROSBY.

Bridgeport, Conn., April, 1904.

THE
FRANCIS E. CLARK YEAR-BOOK

January 1

If you expect little and ask for little, you will get little. As young people advance, they will see new fields to occupy, new heights to scale, new victories to win. If they never try to do a hard thing, they will soon refuse the easiest tasks. If in some respects they fail to do what they have hoped, desired, and even promised to do, they will come far, far nearer to Christ's ideal than if the standards are brought back to the natural level of easy and comfortable mediocrity.

—A Message for the New Year.

January 2

The best way to break with the old is to begin with the new. I have some little purple beeches in my front yard, whose old leaves cling to them still, and rustle in every passing

9

breeze. These old leaves will cling to the trees until in the spring the new leaves push them off. It is very much so with our habits. We must take something into our lives before the old can be expelled. There must be a new life to drive out the old life.

—THE OLD AND THE NEW.

—————

January 3

The great trouble with our New Year's resolutions is that they are often big, hazy, and far off. This year make them definite, specific, relating to things near at hand, things that you can at once put into practice; and, whatever special form they may take with you, let the underlying thought be that of a closer union with Christ, and a stronger effort to bring others to him. Let this be the new endeavor and the new resolution for the happy New Year.

—THE NEW ENDEAVOR FOR THE NEW YEAR.

—————

January 4

But, fathers and mothers, may I not beg of you in Christ's name to help your children up the Hill Difficulty rather than to pull them back? Are you willing to take the responsibility of indifferent, careless, worldly lives, when one ringing call to self-sacrifice might bring your children up to the standard of duty, obligation, and service which Christ himself has planted upon the enemy's ramparts?

—A MESSAGE FOR THE NEW YEAR.

January 5

We are dissatisfied with the past. We are disappointed with ourselves. Our lives have not been the beautiful, strong, cheery lives we dreamed they would be. Last year had altogether too many dark days in it, days of failure and discouragement and sometimes hopelessness. But now a new year is given us; a treasury full of unseen priceless jewels is ours.

In this jewel-box are at least three hundred and sixty-five gems. Indeed, I do not know but it would be nearer the truth to multiply the three hundred and sixty-five by twenty-four, and that again by sixty. But, whatever the number you reckon up, it remains true that the jewel-box of the year is a treasury of untold, undreamed wealth.

—THE JEWEL-BOX OF THE YEAR.

January 6

A beautiful face is only the window of a beautiful soul.

What does it matter if the panes of glass are small, and if the sash is a little crooked, if through the window you see a warm, cosey fireside, a bright evening lamp, happy children at their games, a contented father and mother, well-read books, a full work-basket, a bouquet of fresh flowers, and, in the room beyond, a bountiful supper-table laid for the family?

Is not that a beautiful scene?

These things are symbols of what any face may reveal—happiness, content, intellectual capacity, joy in work, appreciation of beauty, and a generous spirit.

A face that reveals these characteristics cannot be ugly; it cannot be repulsive; it must be attractive and winning; it cannot help being beautiful in the best sense of the word.

—How to be Beautiful, Though Homely.

January 7

When we seek first the kingdom of God, other things will be added. Only when we love the Lord our God with all our might shall we love our neighbors as ourselves.

—Captain Mahan on Personal Religion.

January 8

The Bible leaves us to write our own commentaries. It gives us food for thought, but does not masticate and digest that food for us. It does not furnish what some of the breakfast-food companies advertise—"predigested aliment."
— ALL THINGS.

January 9

God is ready to bless; his promises are sure; his power is omnipotent; his love is almighty. Are we ready to receive the blessing and to carry it to others? That is the only question we have to decide.
—WHAT WE MAY EXPECT.

January 10

Family religion is a foundation-stone of all our religious life in church and state, and family worship lies near the foundation of all family religion. In building the family altar, religion builds itself up.
—TRAINING THE CHURCH OF THE FUTURE.

January 11

A prayer-meeting is as natural and necessary a means of grace to the young Christian as to

the older one. It is as appropriate for the boy
to offer his little prayer to God as for his father
to offer his longer and more comprehensive
petition. It is as proper for the little Christian
to repeat the words of Jesus as for larger Christians to explain them.

—Young People's Prayer-Meetings.

January 12

Good,   strong,   voluntary   expression   of
religious truth in childhood will, we believe,
prevent many of the sad wrecks of religious
faith in manhood.

—Young People's Prayer-Meetings.

January 13

The larger the church, the larger the needs;
the greater the community around about to be
helped, the greater the opportunity for work.
I do not believe that there is a church in all the
world so big that earnest, loyal, devoted Christian Endeavor societies cannot help it to be a
greater and grander church than it otherwise
would be.

—Concerning the Large-Church Problem.

January 14

There is no occasion for framing new excuses: the world, the flesh, and the devil are all busy at this task. The only Endeavor standard is what "Christ would have me do." Let us never lower this, but ever cultivate a more heroic, courageous, conscientious type of Christianity, for this is what the world most needs to-day.

—Some Misapprehensions Corrected.

January 15

To find God, though often he seems to hide himself, is still the great duty of man in this year 1896 after Christ as it was 1896 years before Christ.

Of one thing I am very sure. Impatience, fretfulness, despair, will never find him. Submission, unselfishness, obedience, trust, even in the darkness, will open heaven's door at last. Read over Job's story, dear friends, you who are tempted to "give it all up." The whole book is an answer to the question why men suffer. Read its passages of doubt and deadly fear and hopelessness, and then read the glorious and bright ending of it all; but remember that even in his darkest day Job was able to say, "He knoweth the way I take; when he hath tried me, I shall come forth as gold." Ah! there is the answer to all our questions; there is the justification of all our sufferings. Even your past sin, repented of and forgiven, as well as your other suffering, will refine the gold and purge away the dross.

—The Old, but Ever New, Search.

January 16

All our invitations, warnings, expostulations, pleadings, are for the unconverted. Let me plead with those who are in the inner circle of devoted and joyous service. Now is your accepted time. Now is your day of salvation. "To-day, if ye will hear his voice, harden not your hearts."

—Concerning the Inner Circle.

January 17

Here are we, living with God in our **very** midst; but some of us have never seen him, and others have caught only a fragmentary, fleeting glimpse, and then have turned to our digging and delving in the dirt again.

We have but to lift up our spiritual eyes to behold him, and we have never done it. We hear the noise of his avalanches, the thunder of his providences, and we scarcely turn our heads to see whence the providence comes, or to read its meaning.

O the benumbing effect of familiarity and use! The Bible has been in our hands so many years that it has become a commonplace book to us. We have read its precious promises of rest and comfort so many times that these jewels have lost their sparkle, and are but common pebbles.

We are so used to the thought of God as our refuge and strength, our high rock, our impregnable mountain, that in its familiarity we forget its reality and its tremendous truth.

—A Lesson from the Jungfrau.

January 18

There is a thousand times more music in the song of the birds and the ripple of the brooks than there is in the fiddle of the ballroom. There is vastly more health, wealth, and wisdom, for the genuine soul, with the blue sky for the curtain and the light and shade on forest and river for shifting scenery, than there is in the frescoed theatre with painted trees and rivers and skies for scenery. I would rather walk ten miles into the country for a couple of hours in the silent woods than go across the

street to see a score of people skip up and down
a slippery floor. I should like to have all my
boys—yes, and girls, too—learn to fish, shoot,
row, swim, play baseball, and skate in winter
(I have no great opinion of skating in summer-
time), so that they may grow strong and brave
and sound of heart and limb; but I have no desire to have them spend much time or money
to learn the false graces and poor accomplish-
ments of the dancing-master. Every season
has its outdoor sports and joys; even city boys
can have their share of them. Learn to love
them; and, my word for it, a purer, nobler,
stronger manhood and womanhood will be
yours.   —DANGER SIGNALS.

January 19

The sad, discouraged Christian, who feels
his shortcomings and the degeneracy of the
times in which he lives so overwhelmingly as
to take away his peace and joy, needs to get out
into God's pure air upon some errand of mercy.

—AIDS TO ENDEAVOR.

January 20

"Take down those saints, and coin them into
shillings," once said Cromwell, of the silver

saints in a Catholic cathedral, "and send them about their Master's business." So we need to take down our lofty emotions from the niches they occupy, and send them on some errand of mercy and love.

—The Secret of a Happy Life.

January 21

Certain Scriptures seem to hide their meaning for a time, and flash out on us almost unawares, as the sunlight, long obscured by a cloud, sometimes flashes upon the printed page unexpectedly, as we sit reading with our back to the window.

Thus that expression, "The strength of the hills is His also," never seemed to me to have so much sunlight on it as of late, since I have been looking out daily, hourly, almost every minute, on Pilatus and Rigi and the Stanserhorn, and other Alpine peaks, from our windows in Lucerne and Berne.

The strength of the hills—of these deeply rooted, broad-based mountains that spread out their foot-hills like so many vast outer fortifications of a gigantic fortress—is His also.

The strength of the hills—of these cloud-piercing Alpine summits, snow-clad from January to December, any one of which seems as if, Atlas-like, it could bear the world on its mighty shoulders—is His also.

The strength of the hills—of these vast peaks down which the avalanches roll with thunderous roar, pouring millions of tons of snow and ice into the valleys below—is His also.

The strength of the hills—up many of which man has built his pygmy railway, which seems scarcely to scratch the surface, or make a furrow on their giant crests—is His also.

And all this strength may be ours, Christian Endeavorers, since we are Christ's and Christ is God's. Here we have our warrant for attempting even the impossible. Here, also, we find the assurance of success in every simplest task.

"Trusting in the Lord Jesus Christ for strength," since the strength of the hills is his, and through him ours, there is no duty we need shrink from.

—THE STRENGTH OF THE HILLS.

January 22

Look through the Bible from Genesis to Revelation, and we find it the record of the lives of enthusiastic men; and the Bible is but a transcript of all human history in this respect, for since the world began little that is great and enduring has ever been intrusted to any other than a man of zeal and enthusiasm.

—ENTHUSIASM IN CHRISTIAN SERVICE.

January 23

The soul at peace with God is at peace with itself. The soul at war with God is at war with all mankind.

—HEART TALKS WITH YOUNG MEN.

January 24

It is of no use to strive and struggle and fret and fume. It is of no use to turn the evils out-of-doors unless you open the door to God. God is enough to fill and possess and envelop your life. Fill your thoughts, your affections, your life, with God; then victory and peace will be yours, the enemy will be vanquished, and your joy will be full.

—HEART TALKS.

January 25

I have my impediments, and so have you yours. I am tempted to give up the struggle, and let the impediment win the fight; and so are you. When we do this, our disabilities are likely to make us morose and suspicious and faultfinding, whereas bravely doing our duty, leaving our impediments in the rear, honestly doing the best we can, we in time make for ourselves characters that command the admiration and respect and love of those around us.

Or, to put it in another way, by heroic, loving service Christ's character is formed within us, and his character is always lovable.

Then let us learn this one supreme lesson of Christian Endeavor, to leave our impedimenta behind, and to do the hard things for His dear sake.

—On Doing Hard Things.

January 26

Are you in the inner circle? It is not full. The door is always open. It is your own fault if you stay out. The Holy Spirit has chosen you for membership. The society and the cause of Christ are suffering if you are outside. You know little of the true joy of religion if you are in the outer circle.

—The Inner Circle.

January 27

Undoubtedly there is very much in our temperament and nervous organization to account for the expression or non-expression of religious rapture. We ought to bear this in mind, and not allow ourselves to be too greatly influenced by mere moods.

There is something vastly better than mere rapture, and that is a steady, abiding, peaceful faith; and there is something far worse than depression of spirits or even melancholy, and that is indifference and callousness to Christ's claims and Christ's love.

—DID CHRIST EVER LAUGH?

January 28

The public library as well as the public school is a great unifier. It is one of the crucibles in which the future American nation is being melted and fused. It is one of the educators which makes the new arrival from the steppes of Russia proud of what the Puritans suffered, and of what the Revolutionary fathers achieved. It is a great Americanizer; and while the public school and the public library, and, above all, the church and all its agencies, are doing their work, we need not despair for the future of the republic, even though all Europe casts her ceaseless tides of humanity upon our shores.

—WHAT DO OUR BOYS AND GIRLS READ?

January 29

(PRESIDENT McKINLEY'S BIRTHDAY)

O how much the legacy of this noble Christian life and tranquil death may mean to the young men of America if they will take it to heart! It seems to me it should open the gate of the eternal world to a multitude of the careless and indifferent. It should show the supreme nobility of a Christian life, the absolute serenity of the Christian's death. It should, in revealing the transitoriness of earthly glory, show the eternity of that which is infinitely better than glory—character.

—PRESIDENT McKINLEY'S LEGACY.

January 30

The most dangerous place for any man to reach is the summit of his ambitions.

—A FORWARD LOOK.

January 31

Those that confess Christ before men will not only be confessed by him before their Father, but they will constantly grow in ability and power to do the Father's will, if in a good degree their lives conform to their confessions.

This seems to be practically a universal law in the spiritual world. It is disregarded only at terrible risk of spiritual loss and death.

—THE CHRISTIAN ENDEAVOR MANUAL.

February 1

O, let us always remember that moral disaster comes not from failure to do right or all the good we might, but from unwillingness to get up from defeat and try again.

Our moral fibre begins to disintegrate when we are unwilling to make any fresh resolves, to have any more decision days.

—DECISION THE KEY-NOTE OF ENDEAVOR DAY.

February 2

(CHRISTIAN ENDEAVOR DAY)

The Christian Endeavor Society was born February 2, 1881 in Williston Church, Portland, Maine

No one can realize more fully than I the small part I have had in establishing this society, how largely it has been taken by Providence out of human hands, how spontaneously it has developed; and no one is more grateful that this is not a man-made scheme of Christian nurture, but a God-sent movement.

—TRAINING THE CHURCH OF THE FUTURE.

February 3

In the first place, the Christian Endeavor movement makes for the fellowship and unity of Christians the country over and the world around. It is undoubtedly another tie that binds our hearts in Christian love. The seal of God has been set in a remarkable manner upon this feature of the work. Since he has found a way of promoting loyalty to one's own church and fellowship with those of other folds, can we lightly disregard this road to essential Christian unity which his finger so clearly points out?

—TRAINING THE CHURCH OF THE FUTURE.

February 4

Family religion is a foundation-stone of all our religious life in church and state, and family worship lies near the foundation of all family religion. In building the family altar religion builds itself up.

—THE CHRISTIAN ENDEAVOR MANUAL.

February 5

The covenant pledge, which has been such an important and prominent feature in the history of the Christian Endeavor movement, has this for its purpose: to help every one to serve. The essence of it is really all in its first clause, "Trusting in the Lord Jesus Christ for strength, I promise him that I will strive to do whatever he would like to have me do." The rest is but an amplification of this phrase.

—TRAINING THE CHURCH OF THE FUTURE.

February 6

These efforts, after all, will be but our way, our humble, human fashion, of thinking God's thoughts after him. His salvation is for all. His religion is for the million. He thinks of men in six figures as well as by units. He multiplies the units and tens until they become a million. "No war ever yet was won by mere defence," says Captain Mahan, the brilliant author and devout Christian, "least of all, a war of conquest, which that of Christianity is. Our mission prescribed to us by our Founder, who is our God, is to conquer the world. Warfare, therefore, aggressive warfare in the technical sense, has been our mission since the beginning, bringing to each generation special problems and special conditions." Thank God for this opportunity to work and fight for him. "We are glad we're in this army, and we'll battle for the Lord." —A CONVENTION SERMON.

February 7

One of the ways to keep up with the times and make yourselves felt is to take up one branch, and to make yourself a specialist in this sense, that you can do one thing, at least, better than most other people can do it. The field is too large in these days, and competition is too sharp, for a man to do many things well.

—Our Business Boys.

February 8

I am often asked the question, "Don't you find this constant round of conventions monotonous and wearisome?"

Monotonous! Is a constantly changing panorama monotonous? Is the meeting with old friends monotonous? Is the formation of new friendships wearisome? Is the vision of the ever-advancing kingdom of God among his young people wearisome? Is the growth of Christian Endeavor in faith and beneficence and all activities, and in spiritual depth, monotonous? These are the things that I find in a round of State conventions, and I find them in an ever-increasing measure.

To be sure, there is some weariness to the flesh; there are thousands of miles of travel in

only a fortnight's trip; there are three times
as many addresses as there are days in the
week; and, hardest of all, there is the absence
from home and the breaking up of family life;
but as for the conventions themselves, they are
a constant surprise and joy for their freshness,
brightness, depth, and power.

—A Familiar Letter.

February 9

God is ready to bless. His promises are
sure; his power is omnipotent; his love is almighty. Are we ready to receive the blessing
and carry it to others? That is the only question we have to decide.

—Comrades of the Quiet Hour.

February 10

Young men, make of yourselves evangelists,
while you earn your living in some other way.

—A Familiar Letter.

February 11

But there is something beyond effort, and
that is life; something beyond doing, and that

is being. After a time we feel the need of emphasizing that which lies at the basis of all doing, and we find that it is being. In fact, the more we do, the more surely are we driven back to the source of all right action; for we find that doing cannot long be kept up with genuine earnestness and zeal unless it is the expression of genuine life.

—Concerning Doing and Being.

February 12
(President Lincoln's Birthday)

Lincoln, gaunt, grave, homely, towering Lincoln, the great future hero of the nineteenth century, united with the rarest genius of heart and soul more uncommon common sense than any man of his generation, and for this he will be remembered and loved when other presidents and rulers are but mere names on the pages of dusty history.

—The Great Secret.

February 13

Christianity is a religion of expansive forces. You can no more confine the religion of Christ to old limits than you can grow an oak in a flower-pot. When you confine it, you kill it.

From the time of the first disciples gathered in the upper room, waiting for the Pentecostal blessing, it has been "going and growing."

—A Convention Sermon.

February 14

I am almost tempted to reply that a little devotional reading, like a little learning, is a dangerous thing. Surely the scanty, hasty, hop-skip-and-jump, duty method often leads to distaste for God's Word, and no wonder. But, if my friend will take a good, full half-hour to-morrow morning and every morning for a week, spending at least half of it quietly with his heart open to God for light and guidance, and the other half reading God's morning message to him, with the help, perhaps, of some devout author to illumine the message, I do not think he will ever again find the Bible a dry and uninteresting book.

—Heart Talks with Young Men.

February 15

Find out what you are fitted for; work hard at that one thing; and keep an honest heart.

—Our Business Boys.

February 16

These fundamental and essential principles of the Christian Endeavor Society are, I believe, four and only four: Confession of Christ, service for Christ, fellowship with Christ's people, and loyalty to Christ's church.

—THE CHRISTIAN ENDEAVOR MANUAL.

February 17

Contrast for a single moment the religion of the Bible with the religion of Benares; the temple of the Holy Ghost with the temple of Siva; the stone bull, dirty with the dust and grease of ages, with the Christian's conception of the Lamb of God who taketh away the sins of the world. In fact, the only antidote needed to the claims of the lackadaisical toleration of all religions as equally uplifting to the race is an hour on the Ganges or among the temples of Benares.

—AN HOUR ON THE GANGES.

February 18

A great deal more depends upon what we deem dull, commonplace, and prosaic than upon the occasional lofty mountains of achievement.   —FELLOW TRAVELLERS.

February 19

One test of a truth is that it is universal. Faith is faith in India and Kamchatka. Hope is hope in the New World and the Old. Love is the greatest of these graces at the equator and the poles. So it is in all lesser matters that have in them the elements of universal truth. Here is the test of the value of an idea, of a movement, of an organization.

—The Christian Endeavor Manual.

February 20

I wish that not only every preaching-service, but that every church prayer-meeting and Christian Endeavor service, might close with a quiet moment for silent prayer.

—German Things Worth Copying.

February 21

There is sometimes an outcry against the pledge, as if a mere instrument were exalted to the place of a universal principle. This is not the case. * * * * The pledge is exalted as a painter exalts his brush, as a musician his violin, as a writer his pen. The brush is not the picture; the violin is not the music; the pen is not the poem; but the brush is necessary to the picture, the violin to the music, the pen to the poem, the pledge to the best Christian Endeavor society, because it ensures regular and frequent confession of Christ.

—THE CHRISTIAN ENDEAVOR MANUAL.

———

February 22
(WASHINGTON'S BIRTHDAY)

Most great and strong characters whom God signally uses are at their base modest, shrinking, sensitive. Perhaps we should find that all men who have been most useful were at first self-distrustful, could we but know their early struggles. Surely it was so with Moses, David, Elijah, John the Baptist. The early days of many a modern hero—Cromwell, Washington, Grant—reveal the same characteristic.

—OLD LANTERNS FOR PRESENT PATHS.

———

February 23

Our Bible will not displace or dispute true science, but it alone will make stalwart Christians.

—FELLOW TRAVELLERS.

February 24

There is room even for experiments and failures, since we will always remember that the worst failure is to make no endeavor.

—THE CHRISTIAN ENDEAVOR MANUAL.

February 25

Keep your eyes open; be wide awake; consult those wiser than yourself; and, when you see anything that you can do, do it.

—A FAMILIAR LETTER.

February 26

Shall we spend all our time digging in the scoriæ of the burnt-out emotions of the aged and the middle-aged, and forget the virgin gold-mine of youthful love and enthusiasm, which will so richly reward one's toil?

—PRACTICAL TRAINING IN RELIGIOUS EDUCATION.

February 27

Would you be a friend and have friends? Then practise the presence of God. Seek in him the elements of true friendship. Spend much time with him. Begin the day and close it alone with him. Seek in the likeness and life of Christ the elements which made him the friend of sinners, and you, too, will have learned the art of friend-making.

—THE GREAT SECRET.

February 28

The Bible leaves us to write our own commentaries. It gives us food for thought, but does not masticate and digest that food for us. It does not furnish what some of the breakfast-food companies advertise—"predigested" aliment.

—ALL THINGS.

February 29

(A LEAP-YEAR EXTRA)

The flippant, inane, shallow, or fast girl is about the poorest specimen of human weed that God allows to grow. "A godless woman is an abhorrent creature," says Timothy Titcomb, and he scarcely overstated it.

Look out, my dear masculine moth, and do not get your wings singed, or, worse still, your whole life marred and blighted, by an unworthy love-affair and unhappy marriage.

—HEART TALKS WITH YOUNG MEN.

March 1

Put * * duty before feeling and impulse. * * I should as soon expect to find a magnificent mansion built on the foaming crest of an ocean wave as to see a fine character built on impulse or feeling.

—A FAMILIAR LETTER.

March 2

A fool may advise a philosopher; but it is only a wise philosopher who will heed his advice, even when it is good.

—THE MOSSBACK CORRESPONDENCE.

March 3

If we desire a part in the blessing, we must also have a part in the praying and the giving.

—A FAMILIAR LETTER.

March 4

The minister or Christian worker who is too busy or too pre-occupied to care for the young in the Sunday-school and the young people's society is too busy to build up his church.

—PRACTICAL TRAINING IN RELIGIOUS EDUCATION.

March 5

Nothing that gives us power with men and enables us to lead them on to a better life can be considered small.

—THE MOSSBACK CORRESPONDENCE.

March 6

The grateful soul is not satisfied with speaking its thanks; it wishes to *live* its thanks.

—A FAMILIAR LETTER.

March 7

We have something better than the past to look to; we have the living present.

—CHAIRMAN'S ADDRESS.

March 8

The world does not yet know the supreme attractiveness and love-compelling power of a thoroughly Christlike, thoroughly unselfish, life.

—THE GREAT SECRET.

March 9

No pastor can be too ingenious in setting his young people at work.

—HELPS FOR OUR WORKERS.

March 10

I like to think of the "Captain of our salvation" sometimes as a ship-captain rather than as a military captain. He knows the way, and he steers my bark. The captain of our steamer knows, every day at noon, after he has "taken the sun," just where we are, even within a mile; and I have faith to believe that he will find the little dent on the African coast called Durban harbor, after crossing this great and wide sea, and will take me in safety across the bar. I have the same faith, infinitely increased, in the great Captain; and, when each night comes, I can peacefully go to sleep. He is at the helm. He knows the safe harbor at the end. He will take me across the bar.

—TWENTY-THREE DAYS AT SEA, AND
SOME REFLECTIONS.

March 11

Go by yourself every morning for this infilling of the indwelling God. Know him as a matter, not of books and second-hand information, but of experience. Then you have learned the secret of happiness. As the setting sun lights up the heavens, and makes the darkest clouds radiant with supernal glory, so the happy heart lights up everything upon which the eyes rest.   Niagara becomes more glorious, the home hearthstone more lovely, the Alps more majestic, travel more enchanting, home-staying more charming, success more sweet, sorrow more salutary, and our very tears become prisms through which we behold irradiated the brighter purposes of God.

—The Great Secret.

March 12

Tact, after all, is a spiritual quality.   It may be cultivated.   It comes with a prayerful desire for souls.   —A Familiar Letter.

March 13

If all young men first saw their future life-partners in the prayer-meeting, there would be less work for the divorce courts.

—The Mossback Correspondence.

March 14

Let us get away from the idea that the Quiet Hour is to fit us only for the other world.   Let us rather think of it as a time to acquire power for practical duties and ability for common service.

—A Convention Address.

March 15

Lack of variety in the prayer-meeting is a species of la grippe that is almost fatal.

—A FAMILIAR LETTER.

March 16

God has a right to have a chance at us.

—A QUIET-HOUR ADDRESS.

March 17

You do not wear the same kind of collars and neckties and coats that your grandfathers wore when they were boys, but the same kind of hard work and honesty and truthfulness is necessary for you if you would succeed as most of them succeeded.

—OUR BUSINESS BOYS.

March 18

As there are vast underground rivers in many parts of the world, broader and deeper and of more majestic sweep than any Mississippi or Amazon, streams which men may often tap and bring to the surface in ever-flowing artesian wells, so there is an undercurrent of

happiness in this universe; and, if we connect
our lives with it, our joy is perennial; there
shall be within us then a well of water, spring-
ing up not only unto everlasting life, but to
everlasting happiness. This undercurrent of
happiness, or, rather,—let us give it its nobler
name,—of blessedness, is God.

—CHEER BOOK.

March 19

None of us have, perhaps, Henry Drummond's wit, learning, or natural charm of manner; but we may have the chief quality that
made his character so uplifting an inspiration
to multitudes. I have said much in these letters of late about "the morning watch." I ven-
tured even to recommend in my annual address
at San Francisco the observance of this daily
quiet time alone with God. I know of no other
school than this in which the lesson of Drummond's life can be learned.

— A REMINISCENCE OF PROFESSOR DRUMMOND.

March 20

To-morrow morning rise an hour earlier
than usual. You will be tired and sleepy? No
doubt. You will wish to turn over for another

nap? I do not doubt it. But no matter; overcome drowsy nature for once, at least; and a good hour before breakfast, and before the rest of the family are stirring, be dressed and ready for a talk with the King. The joy of the appointment he is waiting to keep with you is worth the extra exertion a thousand times over.

Take your Bible, your own Bible, the one with marks and references, and comments in your own handwriting, and go, if possible, into a room quite by yourself. Open your Bible to the fourteenth chapter of John, and read a chapter or two from there on, slowly, meditatively, lifting up your heart, and saying frequently as you read, "O Lord, open thou my eyes that I may understand." Perhaps you will not get through half a chapter, so full of new and wondrous meaning will each verse be as you dwell upon it, the new light from heaven illumining the page. No matter. All the better, indeed. The spirit of Christ is in every verse. There is food enough in any verse for a morning meal.

—How Can We Get the Spirit of Christ?

March 21

God calls you to a *definite* service.

—A Familiar Letter.

March 22

The question is not whether card-playing and dancing and theatre-going are damning sins. It is not whether they shut one out of heaven above or the church or Christian Endeavor Society below. The question is whether they promote or hinder the highest type of Christian living; whether they quicken or deaden the spiritual life; whether they open the avenues of the soul to God, or close them to his entrance.

I believe there is only one answer to these questions. One may, perhaps, live a passable religious life, even a Christian life of a certain type, while indulging in these things, I admit; but, if the experience of millions proves anything, it proves that the deeper spiritual life, the life that is hid with Christ in God, cannot be lived while these amusements pre-occupy and engross the soul.

—HEART TALKS WITH YOUNG MEN.

March 23

We desire to accomplish more in this world, to multiply our power to take on more work; and very rightly we desire this. How shall we do it? Only by obtaining more leisure; and this must be leisure from our own nagging, importunate selves, the self that steals our time, and wears out our powers, and makes young men old and strong men sick.

Take time to obtain this leisure. Spend the "morning watch" with God. With open Bible and uplifted heart every day "practise the presence of God." Surrender to him Self, the thief, Self, the robber of time and energy and life itself; sacrifice the self life, and in its place he will give you his life, abundant life; life that has leisure for every duty; life that has abounding vitality; life that is roomy, large, and ample; life that will enable you to take up unattempted tasks and new burdens, and to carry them easily. Make room in your lives for God. Find leisure for him, and he will give you leisure from yourself and for a life-work larger and fuller than you can at first conceive.

—"The Mind at Leisure from Itself."

March 24

What would induce a landsman with a quiet, comfortable home to leave it, and endure the miseries of seasickness twenty-three days on a coolie ship with its filth and its indifferent food, its lukewarm water, its cockroaches, its other vermin that it is still less proper to mention in polite society, and its unutterable smells? What would induce one to do this? Why, the end in view, to be sure, would induce you or me or any of us to take the voyage. If it was our duty, and we could succeed in planting Christian Endeavor a little more firmly in the great African continent, there are few of us who would not start to-morrow. Many times I have thought of South Africa and the work there, and then of the home-going afterwards; and almost every hour has been brightened by present work and pleasant anticipations.

Why should we not brighten our long earthly journey far more than we do with delightful anticipations of the journey's end, and of the work and the home that awaits us?

—Twenty-three Days at Sea and
Some Reflections.

March 25

It is far better to say one thing and stop before remarking, "This reminds me," than it is to be reminded of so many things that at length the clock reminds the audience that it is high time for you to be reminded of nothing further. It is not at all necessary to expound a whole body of divinity in every prayer-meeting, or even to elucidate exhaustively a difficult passage of Holy Writ, and, as for informing the Lord in public prayer so minutely concerning all mundane things, it is much better to ask for one thing that you really want and then have done.

—THE MOSSBACK CORRESPONDENCE.

March 26

There is reason even for experiments and failures, since we will always remember that the worst failure is to make no endeavor.

—LONDON CONVENTION ADDRESS.

March 27

The world is not in such crying need of more ministers and missionaries as it is of better ministers and missionaries.

—HEART TALKS WITH YOUNG MEN.

March 28

Again and again we need to come back to this fundamental thought. The Christian Endeavor movement can prosper only as Christ is in its members and its members are in Christ.

—A WORLD-ENCIRCLING MOVEMENT.

March 29

Giving God a chance at you; that is the meaning of the Quiet Hour. Parents, teachers, friends, books, newspapers, business, pleasure, all these have a chance at us. Should we not also give God a chance at us?

—Convention Speech.

March 30

No one can fairly face the responsibilities of life without asking, prayerfully, "Lord, what wilt thou have me to do?"

—Heart Talks with Young Men.

March 31

Let us not be satisfied with glittering generalities. Abstract propositions have seldom saved a soul or turned the current of a life from self to God.

—A Million Souls for Christ.

April 1

To "get mad" is not only a sign of weakness, but a sign of defeat as well. The successful person can afford to keep his temper and wait for time to vindicate his course.

—The Mossback Correspondence.

April 2

Let us never forget that Christian Endeavor means not only "always at it," but "all at it," as John Wesley said of Methodism, and the more responsibility for service and confession a society puts upon every member, the nearer it comes to the Christian Endeavor ideal.

—How One Society Was Killed and
Another Cured.

April 3

Easter will be a poor, dull day, a day of outward observance and ceremony, a day merely of flowers that fade and music that dies upon the air, unless we know something, each for ourselves, of this "lively hope." This hope is for every one. None is so poorly equipped intellectually, no one has so little imagination or education, no one knows so little of theology or metaphysics, no one is so driven with work or pressed with weariness, that he may not know the joy of Easter, that he may not begin life once more on this day of the "lively hope," having it born within him, and thus being born again to the incorruptible, undefiled, and fadeless inheritance.

—The Day of the Lively Hope.

April 4

Ah! Here is the secret of Easter joy. This is the key to our lively hope. It is realizing the nearness of the unseen One. It is the practising of the presence of God. It is the endurance of every ill, and every sorrow, and every piece of hard routine task-work, as seeing Him who is invisible.

—The Day of the Lively Hope.

April 5

Your victories and mine lie along the same lines, not in the carrying out of all our plans without a break, but in noble purpose, faithful effort, and heroic confidence that God will do his part and turn our seeming success or failure in life, as the case may be, into real and substantial victory.

—A Sermon from the Camera.

April 6

Young men, make money for God. Pledge yourselves to turn your best ability to the making of money, not for a selfish and sordid purpose, but that through your money the world may be evangelized.

—Going and Growing.

April 7

Worldliness, materialism, rationalism, irreverence toward the Word of God, have wrought havoc in some sections. Christian Endeavor has a great mission to do in stemming the tide of worldliness and irreverence, and in holding the young heart of the country sound and faithful to the great central truths of the religion of Jesus Christ.

—An Anticipated Message.

April 8

Worrying, if indulged, gets to be a passion, and, just as some persons, with unconscious irony, say they "enjoy poor health," so there are others who are never quite happy unless they are miserable over some real or imaginary trouble.

—The Mossback Correspondence.

April 9

O, the abiding influence of a good name! "The memory of the just is blessed." The good that men do in humble, quiet ways is not always "interred with their bones," thank God.

—A Sacred Grave.

April 10

Every nail that is driven is better for being clinched.

—THE PASTOR'S FIVE MINUTES.

April 11

Is it possible that you and I have been on a siding all our lives; and even when we thought we were putting on the brakes, and considered ourselves so necessary to keep the train from going to destruction, was it a mere dream and fancy, while in reality the train has gone on and left us without our knowing it?

—THE MOSSBACK CORRESPONDENCE.

April 12

The Endeavorers learn to work by working, as a carpenter learns to build a house, and an artist to paint a picture, and a farmer to till the soil. There is no other way in spiritual character-building or in spiritual vineyard-tilling than the old way, which has been pursued by the gardener and the mechanic from the time of Adam and Tubal-Cain.

—THE CHRISTIAN ENDEAVOR MANUAL.

Bpril 13

Hard usage is the greatest compliment a good book can receive.

—WHAT DO OUR BOYS AND GIRLS READ?

Bpril 14

The father who has a daughter on a missionary field, the brother who has a sister there, does not spare his prayers, or limit his sympathy, or grudge his gifts, for that distant daughter or sister. So, when the Christian Endeavorers fully realize that they have brothers or sisters in all heathen lands, as well as in their own country, their gifts will be poured out more freely, and their prayers will ascend more fervently than ever before.

—THE CHRISTIAN ENDEAVOR MANUAL.

Bpril 15

The idea of tithe-giving is as ancient as the earliest Scriptures. It runs all through the thought of the Old Testament. It was never abrogated in the New Testament; but, if there were no Scripture warrant for it in any part of the Bible, the common sense of practical modern Christians would commend it as a reason-

able and effective means of obtaining the
necessary funds for carrying on the struggle
between the forces of darkness and those of
light.

—THE CHRISTIAN ENDEAVOR MANUAL.

April 16

We seek to enlarge our fellowship, not
chiefly that the Endeavor Society may be
larger, but that the great society of Christ's
friends may be larger.

—A FAMILIAR LETTER.

April 17

I have no quarrel with the ballroom in itself.
I do not know that it is any more sinful in
itself to skip lightly about to the sound of music
than to walk gravely and sedately without any
music to hurry the feet, but I have an undying
and unconquerable prejudice against anything
and everything which will endanger the purity
of young manhood and womanhood. I have
an undying hatred of any place or any amuse-
ment which tends to soil the white lily of maid-
enly modesty; and this, from all that I know,
promiscuous dancing does tend to accomplish.

—DANGER SIGNALS.

April 18

A blundering reader destroys the solemnity which should always attend the reading of the Scriptures.

—AIDS TO ENDEAVOR.

April 19

Can the Ethiopian change his skin? Yes, yes; ten million blood-washed Ethiopians answer, "Yes." This is the "miracle of grace." Salvation consists not in emotion, in hallelujahs, in raptures, in the acceptance of a body of doctrine. It is the whitening of the Ethiopian's skin, the changing of the leopard's inborn spots. It is the learning to do good of those who are accustomed to do evil.

—OLD LANTERNS FOR PRESENT PATHS.

April 20

Why should not our churches have classes for the young, membership in which shall be conditioned not upon age, but upon vital experience in the Christian life? Let the pastor call it the "Church-Preparation Class," and let all children and young people be eligible to it who think they have given their hearts to the Lord Jesus Christ.

—YOUNG PEOPLE'S PRAYER-MEETINGS.

April 21

Young man, if you feel that you have not the moral stamina to break with the companions who are dragging you down, if you feel that there is no other way to throw off this social chain, every link of which is a fetter for your soul, then I beg you to leave everything and flee for your life, though it be to California or Australia or Alaska or Patagonia, though you leave father and mother and home and church behind you, flee as you would flee from the pestilence.

—DANGER SIGNALS.

April 22

Keep healthy bodies, steady nerves, and sensitive consciences, and never be afraid of being too devoted or too religious. The danger is all the other way.

—GOODNESS VERSUS GOODINESS.

April 23

How are you keeping the Quiet Hour? Do you make the most of it? Is it with any of you a dreamy fifteen minutes of hazy, ineffective meditation? Do any of you dawdle over your Bible or your prayers? Do any of you find your thoughts wandering, or else centred upon facts and fancies that are far from the real purpose of the Quiet Hour? * * * I think we should spend a minute or two at least in the realization of the presence of God. * * * Then * * * let us take his own Word and see what message he has for us this very morning—some word of comfort or reproof, of promise or of guidance. I think, too, we should get at least five minutes for reading some stimulating book, at least a page or two each morning, that will illumine our minds and lead us nearer to Him of whom it tells.

—A Quiet-Hour Sketch.

April 24

Our Father is the owner of all, and each one of his children has an undivided share in all the Father's property. All is his; and, if we are his, all is ours as well.

—All Things.

April 25

Life is a very commonplace and practical thing, and it is a good deal better to look at things as they are than to imagine that they are just as we would like to have them.

—The Mossback Correspondence.

April 26

We cannot save up our strength; but, if we use it, we shall receive more, and shall often be surprised at unexpected aid to meet special emergencies.

—THE RENEWAL OF STRENGTH.

April 27

Look backward just long enough to get the courage and inspiration that comes from the thought of God's blessing upon the past, just long enough to see the advancing column and hear their steady tread; and then *forward* to new victories.

—A FAMILIAR LETTER.

April 28

A single truth, a single sentence, from Scripture, has been enough to work revolutions in thought and action, and from age to age the Book loses none of its power over human hearts and lives.

—THE POWER OF GOD'S WORD.

April 29

Let us keep our standard high.

—A FAMILIAR LETTER.

April 30

Forget yourself in working for others. Do not be satisfied to let the sun set any day in the week without having done some act of love *for Christ's dear sake.*

—A Familiar Letter.

May 1

A weed has been described as a plant out of place, and loathsome dirt is frequently good, honest soil in the wrong spot; so whether your wealth is filthy lucre or sparkling gold, whether it furnishes you with weights or wings, depends altogether upon what you do with it.

—The Mossback Correspondence.

May 2

Guerilla warfare never wins any great triumphs. To do our work well within the most narrow horizon, we need to look onward and upward to the stars. To fight with bravest heart any little picket-guard skirmish with the enemy, we need to be inspired by the bugle-call of victory from other divisions of the army.

—A Convention Address.

May 3

A creed in the brain alone is about as worthless a piece of lumber as I can conceive. * * Set your doctrines to work.

—THE MOSSBACK CORRESPONDENCE.

May 4

Every prayer-meeting is a school of Christian service.

—A CONVENTION ADDRESS.

May 5

Find some very small hole into which you can crawl, and there be an inlooker until you can come out and be something more than a critical onlooker.

—THE MOSSBACK CORRESPONDENCE.

May 6

I do not want to have anything better said of me when I join the "great majority" than that some poor friendless man in this world wanted to be near me in heaven, and that heaven would be a little brighter for him thus.

—A CONVENTION ADDRESS.

May 7

There is nothing so practical as an ideal.

—A Convention Address.

May 8

A man who assumes the duties of a moral hose company is a very useless and uncomfortable individual. He rarely puts out a dangerous fire, but is always playing on a useful or innocent one. I would heartily advise you to abandon this business, and see whether you cannot kindle a few fires of righteous zeal in your neighborhood. At least, don't put out your neighbors'.

—The Mossback Correspondence.

May 9

An ounce of experience is worth a pound of theory.

—A Familiar Letter.

May 10

The number of our associate membership ought to be quadrupled, for this is our evangelistic agency.

—An Earnest Appeal.

May 11

The reform shibboleth is not always the watchword of obedience to God. The cheapest kind of popularity can sometimes be won under the banner of reform.

—OLD LANTERNS FOR PRESENT PATHS.

May 12

We know of at least one college boy who was saved from many a sin by the class prayer-meeting to which he early gave his allegiance, and in which he became an active worker. There he committed himself; there he became known as a Christian; and the inconsistency and folly of college rowdyism and wild-oat-sowing never appeared so apparent as in the calm light of the weekly prayer-meeting.

—YOUNG PEOPLE'S PRAYER-MEETINGS.

May 13

There will always be hardened men, men steeped in sin, who have passed beyond the period of Christian nurture, and who must be won, if they are won at all, by the more apparently forceful and startling methods of the evangelist.

—TRAINING THE CHURCH OF THE FUTURE.

May 14

He who in love and lowliness looks into God's face at length is seen to have in his own face the love and gentleness and grace of God, and the peace which passeth understanding.

—THE GREAT SECRET.

May 15

We exalt the pledge as a builder exalts his plumb-line and spirit-level. They are not his house, but he cannot build his house without them.

—LONDON CONVENTION ADDRESS.

May 16

There is a peculiar fragrance about unpaid service for the Master, which I believe is most grateful to him. O, let us not allow the mercenary spirit to creep into our most holy things.

—THE FRAGRANCE OF UNPAID SERVICE.

May 17

The Lord does not help the lazy and shiftless church out of its difficulties, any more than the lazy, shiftless grocer.

—WAYS AND MEANS.

May 18

Meekness is compounded of love, patience, gentleness, strength, and self-forgetfulness; and I think the last quality predominates. The meek man bows his head, but he bows it only to God; he bends his back, but he bends it to carry another's load.

—An Unpopular Virtue.

May 19

Treat the presence of God as you treat any other great fact; only remember that this is the most stupendous and momentous of all facts. That God is in the world, the Bible, history, and the consciousness of millions teach us. Why not accept this fact and live in its light?

—A Familiar Letter.

May 20

There is one secret, and only one secret, of communion with the infinite One. "The pure in heart shall see God." The foul in heart, the deceitful, the dishonest, the selfish, the worldly-minded, the envious, and malicious cannot see God. Their sins like a thick cloud blot him out.

—The Dying Gambler's Lesson.

May 21

Woe unto the young man who will not be warned by the experience of others, but who ventures to play with the very teeth of destruction.

—THE MOSSBACK CORRESPONDENCE.

May 22

He who hath come to our aid in every time of need will not, if we are faithful and humble, desert us in any extremity.

—GOD'S PROVIDENCES.

May 23

Keep your conscience unwarped and tender, and then with prayer take every doubtful matter to that tribunal, and you will not go far wrong.

—WAYS AND MEANS.

May 24

A smile is not a smirk. A real smile is not an expression put on. The genuine smile must come from the genuinely happy heart. * * * The lake cannot help reflecting the sky; the Christian who is living the life he ought to live cannot help showing forth the love of Christ.

—A FAMILIAR LETTER.

May 25

I cannot keep your conscience, or you mine. I know what is wrong for me; you know what is wrong for you. No matter what others do or do not do. What you are doubtful about, as to whether it is right or wrong, is wrong for you until you have decided that it is right. Then go ahead and do it, whatever others say, if you have no secret qualms, and if you can ask and have asked God's blessing upon that thing.

—WAYS AND MEANS.

May 26

I am daily more and more convinced that the difference between success and failure in life depends upon a very narrow margin of excellence.

—WAYS AND MEANS.

May 27

The Christlike spirit always looks out through beautiful eyes. Christ's smile always rests on beautiful lips. The secret of beauty, would you know it? It is the same as the secret of health. Practise the presence of God.

—THE GREAT SECRET.

May 28

It is a sad thing for that soul that has not fitted itself to take up God's work when God calls him to it.

—A Familiar Letter.

May 29

The true patriot is the one who tries to stop the disease before the whole body politic is sick and sore.

—Fellow Travellers.

May 30

(Memorial Day)

The consecrated patriot will read the history of his country, learn its lessons, and will see God on every page.

—Consecrated Patriots.

May 31

Let us widen the scope of our prayers until they take in our brothers and sisters in all the world.

—A Familiar Letter.

June 1

I often think, almost with a shudder, of the boy who goes out from his father's house into the impurity of the street and the school. He has been most carefully reared; every evil thing has been kept beyond his reach; he has been loved and guarded and prayed for; but yet one half-hour with the bad companion, one glance at the lewd picture, and the careful training of years is forgotten; and the leper, entering through Eye-door or Ear-door, has taken up his abode in that pure young soul, and is only too ready to open the door over and over again to his loathsome companions, until at last little is left but corruption and death in that heart which left the father's house white and unsullied.

—DANGER SIGNALS.

June 2

The ability and willingness to express one's convictions is almost as vital to the Christian life as the possession of convictions. There are thousands and tens of thousands of Christians in our churches whose whole development has been stunted because they have never given utterance to that which is struggling within them.

—YOUNG PEOPLE'S PRAYER-MEETINGS.

June 3

There is a homely old New England word spelled g-u-m-p-t-i-o-n, which stands for a capital quality greatly needed by every committee as well as by every individual. I do not need to define it; but, when this quality is accompanied by devotion and zeal and prayer, any of these committees that the church needs cannot fail to do a noble work for the church.

—A FAMILIAR LETTER.

June 4

How insignificant is every worker in comparison with the work!

—A FAMILIAR LETTER.

June 5

Character is a plant of slow growth, and he who hacks at this tree destroys what years cannot replace.

—DANGER SIGNALS.

June 6

Good, strong, voluntary inspiration of religious truth in childhood will, we believe, prevent many of the sad wrecks of religious faith in manhood.

—AIDS TO ENDEAVOR.

June 7

Whatever reaches one heart is apt to reach another. Whatever helps one life is pretty sure to help another.

—OLD LANTERNS FOR PRESENT PATHS.

June 8

Don't spoil a good housekeeper to make a poor poetaster, or waste the energies of a good Christian in mediocre sentimentalism.

—THE MOSSBACK CORRESPONDENCE.

June 9

Do not overwork the story of Gideon and his three hundred. It does not teach that God prefers to work with the few rather than the many. Ten thousand Gideonites are better than three hundred; only see that they are Gideonites.

—A CONVENTION ADDRESS.

June 10

Because it is so much easier to bend the twig than the full-grown tree, this does not prove that it is not necessary to bend the twig.

—TRAINING THE CHURCH OF THE FUTURE.

June 11

Let us not call our obstinacy firmness, or our mulishness resolution. Any goat can beat us in the pastime of butting against a stone wall; and in the feat of standing still because other people want us to move forward, any donkey or pig can easily surpass us. It isn't worth while to compete with the lower animals at their own tricks.

—THE MOSSBACK CORRESPONDENCE.

June 12

"Practising the presence of God." It involves going away by one's self. It involves a daily quiet hour with God. It involves a putting away of all known sin. It involves a searching of the heart for the rebellious life-guard who would keep some of the apartments of the soul closed to the entrance of the King.

—THE GREAT SECRET.

June 13

The modest man that yet dares to speak for God and do the right has always been God's chosen man.

—OLD LANTERNS FOR PRESENT PATHS.

June 14

The churches that are satisfied with their own culture, or their own ritual or doctrine, and do not seek to win others to the standard of Christianity, have soon become paralyzed or atrophied.

—A CONVENTION ADDRESS.

June 15

Every hand-shake is a good seed; every smile is another. There is nothing more catching than good nature. * * * The seed you sow will show itself one of these days.

—THE MOSSBACK CORRESPONDENCE.

June 16

A limp Bible in the hands is an excellent thing; but it is robbed of something of its power when it goes with a limp collar, a greasy waistcoat, or a beard of four days' growth.

—THE GREAT SECRET.

June 17

Our society ought to develop character by encouraging everywhere and always the heroic spirit.

—A FAMILIAR LETTER.

June 18

Why should we not brighten our long earthly journey far more than we do with delightful anticipations of the journey's end and of the work and the home that awaits us?

—Twenty-three Days at Sea.

June 19

Put more inside your skull and less outside; invest to-morrow in a new book instead of a new necktie.

—The Mossback Correspondence.

June 20

We do not worship our pledge; but we simply say that this is a way that God has shown us whereby we can satisfy the longings of our hearts for better service.

—A Convention Address.

June 21

I never saw a nut of any kind that was not enclosed in a shell; and usually the harder the shell, the sweeter the nut. A nut that isn't worth cracking isn't worth eating.

—The Mossback Correspondence.

June 22

Let us bring our minds back to the one plain, indisputable fact which the history of every human soul reiterates. There is but one being large enough to fill the soul of the puniest man. It is God.

There is but one supreme aim, the attainment of which means success. It is God.

There is but one life-purpose worth achieving. It is God.

—The Great Secret.

June 23

If Christian Endeavor is good for you and me, it is good for some one else who hasn't got it yet.

—A Convention Address.

June 24

How can you expect to raise up an active Christian worker without the preparatory training-place where Christian work is done? It is not enough that the engineer should have studied about the locomotive from books; he must be actually in the shop where it is made, and work it before he is fitted to run it. We expect our Christian boys and girls one of these days to be Christian men and women, and we expect them to assume the duties of Christian men and women. Can they do this if they only know about these duties in a theoretic way, and not at all by practice and experience?

—Young People's Prayer-Meetings.

June 25

Of all human disagreeables, the man who receives courtesies and favors, and never acknowledges them, is one of the most unpleasant; appreciation of welcome and courtesy, of bed and board, and of the numberless, nameless attentions which a kind host bestows, is the best current coin in payment of hospitality.

—Guests—and Guests.

June 26

"One family we dwell in Him,
One church, above, beneath."

No one ever gave a broader or truer definition of the church than Charles Wesley sung in those familiar lines. It would have been well if the church had never adopted a narrower one. The church is the family of God.

—What the Y. M. C. A. Has Done for the Church.

June 27

Every one should set before himself a high ideal, and then seek to become a powerful magnet to attract all others to that ideal.

—The Great Secret.

———

June 28

Health lies very near the foundation of happiness and prosperity and beauty.

—The Great Secret.

———

June 29

There is always a danger in religious work of making an end out of a means, of getting so interested in the road that we shall forget the goal.

—A Familiar Letter.

———

June 30

We all have to struggle with our advantages quite as much as with our disadvantages, with our gifts quite as much as with our defects.

For instance, the pretty girl must guard against the vanity and conceit and love of praise which good looks often generate. The muscular young athlete must see to it that his health and strength do not make him an overbearing bully.

The nimble-witted man is in danger of being supercilious and offensive toward slower-paced mortals.

The fluent minister is in ceaseless danger of the "fatal facility of utterance," lest the gift of speech become the gift of gab.

—WRESTLING WITH OUR ADVANTAGES.

July 1

No one can walk over those mounds, or see those eloquent tablets or monuments, without praying, "From fratricidal war, O God, forever deliver us."

—GETTYSBURG FORTY YEARS AFTER THE WAR.

July 2

This faculty of seeing the best in others involves a good deal more than at first appears.

It implies humility and modesty, for a man who thinks of himself more highly than he ought to think will be sure to think of others less highly than he ought.

It implies that he is not self-centred or selfish, for one who is always thinking how much better he himself could do or say the same thing, will not be likely to see the best in others.   —LESSONS FROM THE LIVING.

July 3

The fact that needs to be made very plain is that the body comes in time to express the character, accurately, exactly, inevitably. The beautiful soul must in time come to look out through beautiful eyes. The beautiful character is sure to express itself, sooner or later, in a beautiful smile, in a charming expression, that makes the whole face lovely.

—THE GREAT SECRET.

July 4

A man cannot be the best kind of Christian without being a patriot. If you never to yourself have said, "This is my own, my native land," especially on the great national anniversaries, you should suspect the genuineness of your religion, as well as your love of country.

On the fourth of July let every American Endeavorer dedicate himself anew to his country as well as to his Lord, to God and home and native land.

—RELIGION AND PATRIOTISM.

July 5

This art of reading is by no means an unmixed blessing; indeed, it may be an unmixed curse unless we read the right books.

—THE ART OF READING: A BLESSING OR A CURSE?

July 6

There is no other test of the value of a fruit-tree than fruit-bearing. It has no other reason for existence. No more has a Christian. If a fig-tree does not bear figs, it is absolutely worthless as a fig-tree. If a Christian bears no fruit of a good life and kindly deeds, he is worthless as a Christian. "Herein is my Father glorified," said Christ on another occasion, "that ye bear much fruit." No excuse will avail; no substitute will answer; nothing but fruit can justify a Christian's existence.

—RELIGIOUS BARRENNESS.

July 7

Two weeks of travel are as good for young men and women who keep their eyes open and their souls responsive as a term in the university.

—HOW CONVENTIONS PAY.

July 8

To learn to play when playtime comes is as important as to learn to work the other fifty weeks out of the fifty-two, and a more important lesson, even, for some Americans to learn.

—Down the Rhine in a Freight Steamer.

July 9

Confess, repent, forsake sin; and the darkness will flee away, and God's light will flood your soul.

—How to Get Rid of Sin.

July 10

Professions are useless unless the life corresponds. If we live in sin, and still profess to be in fellowship with God, we lie; that is all there is to it.

—How to Get Rid of Sin.

July 11

If anything can make the angels weep, it seems to me that it must be the bloodshed and carnage of an awful battle.

—Endeavorers, War Against War.

July 12

Vacation time is the best test of our Christian characters.

—A Familiar Letter.

July 13

The question is not what is popular, but what is right.

—Old Lanterns for Present Paths.

July 14

With God in the heart sin flees, as the darkness disappears before the electric light. With sin cherished in the heart God withdraws and darkness reigns.

—How to Get Rid of Sin.

July 15

Many a man has been happy in prison. Many another has sung praises at the stake. Thousands have been serenely placid while a cancer was gnawing at their vitals.

Why? Were they not miserable? O yes, their bodies were in misery; but they were yet happy with a joy that close prison walls could not crush, nor blazing fagots burn, nor consuming cancer eat away, because the soul is not the body, and the soul is the man. Here is an argument for immortality. Here is a body-blow at materialism—the fact proved by tens of millions of the living and the dead that a man may be·happy though miserable.

—How to be Happy, Though Miserable.

July 16

No face can be so plain that it may not be beautiful if through it show glints of happiness, content, intellect, generosity.

—How to be Beautiful, Though Homely.

July 17

A boy of twelve to-day is just as old and just as young as a boy of twelve in the former days. A young man of twenty to-day is just onescore years of age, and is no older or younger, dear reader, than you or I were when we were twenty years of age. He needs the same training, will respond to the same appeals; he will be inspired by the same hero-isms, that moved our hearts ten or twenty or thirty years ago.

—The Buoyant Young Life of the Present.

July 18

To practise the presence of God is to grow beautiful in face.

—THE GREAT SECRET.

July 19

Why are we banded together? Why do we keep the Quiet Hour? Only that we may receive a blessing in our own hearts? Only that we may know the joy of communion with God? Yes, for this, and for much more—even that we may bring a blessing upon others, that we may offer the fervent, effectual prayer that availeth much.

—COMRADES OF THE QUIET HOUR.

July 20

There is just one person in the world who has your work to do, and she is called by your name. There is one place that no one of the millions of young women of America can fill except yourself. You can, to be sure, so dwarf and stunt yourselves that you may fill no useful place, but it will not be God's fault or nature's fault. You have every natural aptitude needed.

—A YOUNG WOMAN'S RIGHTS.

July 21

A young woman too often takes up some employment as an expedient to kill time until Prince Charming appears, riding over the plains to claim his own. Next to having no aim is it to have this temporary expedient and time-killer for an object in life. Prince Charming may come; very likely he will; but it will be all the better for him and for her if he finds the object of his search honestly and patiently doing some one thing for which she has fitted herself, rather than nervously starting up at every ring of the doorbell, thinking that it marks the advent of the prince.

—Looking Out on Life.

July 22

Not only is it true that a beautiful act is itself beautiful; but, often repeated, it makes beautiful the character, and eventually the face, of the doer.

—The Great Secret.

July 23

The Christian Endeavor constitution is no hard chrysalis which forever keeps the butterfly within from trying its wings.

—A Convention Address.

July 24

O brave, strong, modest, undaunted spirit! May we learn thy secret of uncompromising, unswerving allegiance to the Lord of hosts. May we dare to be Jeremiahs. May we dare to stand alone against a hostile world, if need be, the Lord our only fortress and high tower.

—OLD LANTERNS FOR PRESENT PATHS.

July 25

If your capital in life is only a pleasant smile, a soft voice, a bright face, a winning manner,—and none to whom I speak have less,—use them, every one, and use all you have, but use your own. Do not try to acquire the smile and voice and manner of some one else. If you do, you will simper instead of smile; you will make eyes instead of shooting dangerous glances; and you will really repel when you intend to attract.

—A YOUNG WOMAN'S RIGHTS.

July 26

Love, let us remember, is something more than a sentiment. Here is where the fatal mistake is most often made in domestic life. The sentiment and poetry of love is all very well in its place. I would not decry it or undervalue it, but I say that it is altogether worthless if it cannot stand the test of the wear and tear of every day.

—Looking Out on Life.

July 27

"Go to work," said the famous English doctor to his rich, dyspeptic patient; "go to work. Live on sixpence a day, and earn it."

"Go to work," says the wise Physician of souls to him who would escape this worst of all spiritual diseases. The sad, discouraged Christian, who feels his shortcomings and the degeneracy of the times in which he lives so overwhelmingly as to take away his peace and joy, needs to get out into God's pure air upon some errand of mercy.

—Young People's Prayer-Meetings.

July 28

Whenever instruction is substituted for inspiration, whenever the head takes the place of the heart, whenever a Bible class, most important as these are, takes the place of prayer-meetings, loss and dearth follow. Give

the Bible class its place, but not the place of
the prayer-meeting. Let that be sacred to
communion with God, pleading with God,
listening to God, and familiar, unconstrained
intercourse with fellow Christians.

—SHALL THE PRAYER-MEETING BE ABANDONED?

July 29

The influences of a good home can never be
confined within four walls.

—LOOKING OUT ON LIFE.

July 30

The bacillus of every national disease that
ever decimated a people is the same. The
source of every national disaster can always be
spelled with three letters, s-i-n. "Your sins
have withholden good from you."

—OLD LANTERNS FOR PRESENT PATHS.

July 31

It is hard to deceive your fellow men, and
still harder to deceive the angels.

—THE MOSSBACK CORRESPONDENCE.

August 1

After all is said, the spirit of a man is the man. He may say this or that; he may make a mistake now and then; he may be gruff, and perhaps unsocial; he may wear a shaggy coat outside; but, when we can find out his spirit, his animating purpose, we have found out the man. He may be homely and awkward and poor and ill dressed and uncouth; but beneath the dress and the manners and the face there is always something else that we need to inquire about, and this is that intangible, inexplicable, but very real, thing called the spirit of the man.

—WHY I LIKE NORTHFIELD.

August 2

Bossism is quite as offensive in social and family life as in politics, and even more uncomfortable.

—THE MOSSBACK CORRESPONDENCE.

August 3

Fishing is good for a recreation, but it is not well for too many to take it up as the serious and only business of life. There is much poetry surrounding the rippling trout-stream on the summer morning, with the whispering woods and glimpses of blue sky overhead, and the romantic vistas of forest before and behind; but I imagine that the poor fellows on the Grand Banks who do nothing but fish for a living find it dreary and often hopeless and unproductive toil. I am very sure that young women who have no resources within themselves, no independence of character, and no other means of employment except fishing for a husband in the whirlpool of society, must often be miserable and heartbroken. If they make this their sole business in life, too, they do not often succeed very well; but, while hoping to hook a leviathan, they often catch a gudgeon or a very small sprat.

—A Young Woman's Rights.

August 4

I have all honor for the worn mother whose pale cheek and wrinkled brow tell of loving vigils and constant care for loved ones, but I have no honor or respect for the aimless, lackadaisical young person whose pale cheek tells only of chalk and slate-pencils and chocolate creams and late hours. There is nothing interesting or pathetic about her.

—Looking Out on Life.

August 5

Much that goes by the name of success is not worthy of the name. Success is not money-getting. The rich man may be a pitiful failure. The poor man may be a grand success. It is possible to buy gold too dear and political honor too dear. True success is the attainment of a worthy ideal without the least sacrifice of honor or manliness.

—DANGER SIGNALS.

August 6

Hustle and strenuousness seem to win all the prizes of the twentieth century, and it is high time that every effort should be made to recover what has been called "the lost art of meditation," to set up a bulwark, if possible, between the young soul and the commercial, materialistic flood, which would be likely to overwhelm it, to teach a multitude of Christian Endeavorers that the things which are seen are temporal and the things which are unseen are eternal.

—THE CHRISTIAN ENDEAVOR MANUAL.

August 7

There is something more to a gentleman than a gloved hand and a polished shoe, an immaculate coat and a suave manner. No person can be truly polite who is not a lady or gentleman at heart, who is not ready at all times to do a kind deed for others out of a genuine interest in and regard for them.

—THE MOSSBACK CORRESPONDENCE.

***

August 8

There is nothing so foreign to a true woman's nature as worldliness, godlessness. In a man it is unnatural, hardening, and debasing; in a woman it is atrocious and horrible. As much as her finer nature raises her nearer the angels, so the deadening and blunting of this nature brings her nearer the devils than a man often falls.

—A YOUNG WOMAN'S WRONGS.

***

August 9

If you are not a confessing Christian, a working Christian, a loyal Christian, a consecrated Christian, there is something the matter with your foundations. You need to look to them; for, when the rains descend, and the floods come, and the winds blow, your Christian character and life may be swept away. But the movements that are built upon principles, the societies which are based upon these foundations, the individuals that are thus rooted and grounded, need have no anxious fear. They fall not, for they are founded upon a rock.

—THE IMPORTANCE OF FOUNDATIONS.

August 10

True politeness, after all, is a matter of the heart rather than of conventionalities.

*   *   *   *   *   *

You cannot make a brass coal-scuttle into a silver vase by rubbing the outside with silver-polish.

—THE MOSSBACK CORRESPONDENCE.

August 11

Better never learn your letters than to read about unholy love, and seduction, and divorce, and the horrible sins that are gilded and painted white in these miserable novels. Shun all this class of stuff as you shun leprosy. Better have the leprous scales on your face, where they will only ruin physical beauty and comeliness, than have them on the heart, where they will ruin the purity of the soul.

—LOOKING OUT ON LIFE.

August 12

The failure of every society that has failed, so far as I know, can be traced directly to a lack of the prayer-meeting pledge.

—Ways and Means.

August 13

There is a duty devolving upon every Christian, not only to see that his heart is right, but that the windows through which the world looks in upon him are clear and transparent.

—The Mossback Correspondence.

August 14

The boy from the country, with the cowhide boots and homespun jacket and uncouth manners, if he has integrity, good habits, and a strong will on his side, is far more likely to succeed than the city-bred boy who lacks these qualities. The dude, with his arms akimbo, and ivory-headed cane, even if he plasters his hair upon his forehead in the most approved style, finds very soon that these graces are not the open sesame of business prosperity; and the rougher, sterner, more manly virtues are thus often developed at the expense of the gentleman.

—A Young Woman's Wrongs

August 15

Decide what you ought to do as a young Christian. Do not be laughed or browbeaten out of your convictions. Lift up your banner, and stand to your colors.

—A BIRTHDAY MESSAGE.

August 16

You cannot grow strong without soul-food any more than your muscles can be developed on a starvation diet.

—A FAMILIAR LETTER.

August 17

O young women! would that some word of mine might show you how a whole-hearted consecration to Christ glorifies and ennobles your treasure of womanhood. It does for the jewel of your life what the lapidary does for the rough, unsightly stone from the diamond mine; it makes it glow with a heavenly light. There is nothing so distorted and perverted and deformed as a godless womanhood; there is nothing so beautiful and precious as a godly womanhood.

—A YOUNG WOMAN'S WRONGS.

August 18

There is no other way in which a Christian can better show his devotion than by attendance, even at personal inconvenience, on the services of the church.

—WAYS AND MEANS.

August 19

Don't make a cloak of your modesty and diffidence to keep you from doing a duty; such a cloak is apt to prove the shroud of many a good deed.

—THE MOSSBACK CORRESPONDENCE.

August 20

A happy day is but the reflection of a happy spirit, and the happy spirit is the reflection of the Spirit of God shining upon the soul.

—A FAMILIAR LETTER.

August 21

Do be cordial in your manner. A cold-blooded fish is very well in the sea or in the refrigerator, but I should never think of shaking hands with it.

—THE MOSSBACK CORRESPONDENCE.

August 22

If your companion, though he be your best friend, cause you to stumble; if he leads you into bad ways; if he makes you careless and thoughtless, and indifferent of the good, and complacent of the evil, cast him off, flee from him as Joseph fled out of the way of temptation, though you leave the very garment by which he seeks to hold you in the clutches of the tempter.

—Danger Signals.

August 23

There is no abiding without meditation and communion.

—"More Fruit."

August 24

The Christian Endeavor Society is not a "sprinter" that can make a hundred-yard dash and beat all competitors; it is a steady-going, summer-and-winter, day-in-and-day-out society. It was established for constant service, not for a spurt, nor for a few extra galvanic twitches of life once in a while. The test of any society is not what it does once in a great while, but what it does fifty-two weeks of the year.

—Ways and Means.

August 25

I have about made up my mind to live in the present instead of the past, to do what little I can to make the passing days better instead of groaning over the departure of the "good old times."

—THE MOSSBACK CORRESPONDENCE.

———

August 26

Make stepping-stones of your difficulties and obstacles to the largest successes in the kingdom of God.

—A SICK-BED FOR A THEME.

———

August 27

The world cannot be regenerated without the help of brave women as well as of brave men. It has been too long thought that courage was the prerogative of a man, virtue or purity of a woman. We shall never reach the true plane from which we can all together, men and women, with united effort lift up humanity, until we realize this truth, that a man must be pure as well as brave, and a woman must be brave as well as pure.

—LOOKING OUT ON LIFE.

August 28

You cannot make much of a hero out of a hired Hessian. Cowardice is almost always the sister of Aimlessness.

—LOOKING OUT ON LIFE.

August 29

It is a delightful thing to be a good singer, a God-given talent to be prized and cultivated; it is worth much to be a good conversationalist, to have a genial disposition, a cordial manner; but we must allow God to have control of them all as ministering spirits to lead us upward, and not let the devil use them as his henchmen to drag us down.

—DANGER SIGNALS.

August 30

I know of no better remedy for wandering thoughts than to fix them upon God's word to us. After a little we shall hear his voice speaking to us, even in a more direct and intimate relation still; and, while the printed word becomes no less precious, we shall listen to his immediate interpretation of it, and rejoice greatly in the realization of his nearness.

—A FAMILIAR LETTER.

August 31

Let us never be tempted to ignore or discard our foundation principles. Let us never make light of our covenant pledge or that for which it stands; for it is no mere formula, or prescription, or form of words. It is the rock foundation of confession, service, loyalty, and consecration to Christ and the church, without which the society could never exist.

—THE IMPORTANCE OF FOUNDATIONS.

September 1

Our vacation has done us little good unless we have come back from it healthier and heartier than we went away.

—WAYS AND MEANS.

September 2

There should be no drones in the Christian Endeavor hive. Every Endeavorer should do something definite to advance the cause of Jesus Christ. We should all be brave, true, consistent, and faithful; and we should not be afraid to attempt great things.

—A NEW ZEALAND ADDRESS.

September 3

Every day you stay outside the ranks of God's people is in some sense a wasted day.

—WAYS AND MEANS.

September 4

The roots of the Christian Endeavor tree wherever it grows are confession of Christ, service for Christ, fellowship with Christ's people, and loyalty to Christ's church.

—LONDON CONVENTION ADDRESS.

September 5

The appreciative man sees God in everything. He understands the blessings in his surroundings, and does not overestimate his ills. He finds twice the comfort in life that he otherwise would. He can almost extract sunshine from cucumbers. He can certainly find joy in the snow and in the rain, in the cloud and in the sunshine.

In each springtime and harvest there is great, rich, new blessing. In every commonplace scene, in every ordinary event, there are new comfort and grace for the man who can see God in them.

—ON SEEING THE UNSEEN.

September 6

It is said that the greatest vices are only the greatest virtues perverted, and I suppose it is also true that the little failings which injure your usefulness and mine are often but the perversion of some otherwise admirable trait of character.

—The Mossback Correspondence.

September 7

Eminent respectability cannot reach the heart of a little child, cannot quiet the fluttering pulse of the dying sinner, cannot bring the Magdalen up to its own serene level. It is all very admirable when mixed in due and just proportions with earnest love to Christ, and unflagging devotion to the souls for which Christ died; but it is a very poor and barren substitute for either.

—The Mossback Correspondence.

September 8

The Young People's Society of Christian Endeavor is simply an organized effort to lead the young people to Christ and into his church, to establish them firmly in the faith, and to set them at work in the Lord's vineyard.

—Ways and Means.

September 9

If all Americans were McKinleys, how the rough corners of life would be smoothed off, and the sum total of human happiness be increased! I believe that his life and death will do not a little to exalt the milder virtues of gentleness, kindliness, and chivalric courtesy.

—PRESIDENT MCKINLEY'S LEGACY.

———

September 10

I must say I do not find myself placed in an enviable light in comparison with my dog in the way I receive chastisement.

It has taken me months and years to acknowledge that some border-land sins were sins at all; and, when I have been chastised by Providence for working too late at night, or worrying too much, or exercising too little, or for eating what did not agree with me, I have not taken my medicine peaceably and humbly, but have been rebellious and unreasonable, and thought hard of Providence.

But my dog has been willing at once to kiss the hand that struck him. Well, well, I am just an "ornery man," as the crackers in Florida would say. I must learn a lesson from my collie.

—THE CONFESSIONS OF A COLLIE'S MASTER.

September 11

He was not always right, but he always meant to be right.

—At Gladstone's Bier.

September 12
(Dr. Clark's Birthday)

How good is a new beginning, a new day, a new year, a new birthday, a new term at school, a new twelvemonth of work!

We can leave the old, imperfect past behind us.

We can turn the old, blotted page, and begin a new record on a fresh page.

We can forget the things that are behind. We can press forward.

—A Familiar Letter.

Birthdays are worth celebrating. If the year has been lived well, each one is a little better worth celebrating than the last.

—Christian Endeavor Day.

I am sorry for the man who makes no use of anniversaries, whether they mark his own birthday or the century's.

—A Forward Look.

September 13

I am coming to think more and more of the art of appreciation. I believe it would do more to sweeten and brighten life than almost any art we could learn.

If it is more blessed to give than to receive, the blessedness that comes next is that of knowing how to receive graciously.

—APPRECIATION AS A FINE ART.

September 14

Find out and enjoy every one's best points, and in some sense they will become yours; for the appreciative person comes in a measure into possession of every good thing he appreciates.

—APPRECIATION AS A FINE ART.

September 15

Do not forget to make some allusion to that happy hour you spent in prayer and Bible-reading last week; and, if I were you, I would write out in black and white the good resolutions with which I began the new year, and then read them over on the thirty-first day of next December.

—THE MOSSBACK CORRESPONDENCE.

September 16

If your tongue is a Damascus blade, sharpened on both edges, use it sparingly and cautiously; let your raillery be good-natured; laugh with people rather than at them, and they will love you all the better for it.

—The Mossback Correspondence.

September 17

Christian Endeavor stands for a definite purpose and a direct aim.

—A Convention Address.

There is a busyness which is not business. There is an activity which is the veriest idleness, and that is the kind of idleness I most fear for you.

—Looking Out on Life.

September 18

There is a Christian womanhood for the most lowly and shrinking; and beyond this, if you comprehend all that the words imply, there is no higher destiny for a seraph or an archangel.

—Looking Out on Life.

September 19

I wonder if any one will read this chapter who feels that his own manhood is being undermined, that he is one of the serfs, that he is in the chain-gang, that his master is King Alcohol.

Let me tell any one who feels in this way of another King, a stronger King than King Alcohol, a King with more subjects and larger revenues and mightier power. I know not how you can escape from King Alcohol except by transferring your allegiance to this King. Your will is weak; home influences are unavailing; even a mother's prayers and sobs you forget; your pledge will be broken; the antidote that you take will not quench your thirst. This King will be by your side in every trying hour of temptation. He will break your shackles. He will rescue you from the clutches of the enemy. He will never leave you nor forsake you. His name is Jesus Christ.

—Danger Signals.

September 20

Our covenant—a definite way of doing definite things at a particular time for Jesus' sake.

—A Convention Address.

September 21

No rules can be laid down that are equally applicable to all, for the Father has allowed different souls to approach him through different channels. A towering mountain, a placid lake, a stretch of peaceful, quiet meadow-land, might lead many a soul to God, as the sight of the apparently lifeless tree in the winter-time led that remarkable monk, Friar Lawrence, to a sense of the power and presence of God in all things.

—THE CHRISTIAN ENDEAVOR MANUAL.

September 22

If the gas leaks, let us stop the leak instead of blowing up the gas-house. If the train is late, let us get to our destination just as soon as possible, instead of anathematizing the railroad and refusing to get aboard when the train does come along. If the times are bad, let us mend them, instead of groaning over the departure of the past and growling over the coming of the present, for our lamentations will neither bring back yesterday nor delay the coming of to-morrow.

—THE MOSSBACK CORRESPONDENCE.

September 23

Every prayer-meeting is a school of Christian service.

—A Convention Address.

In the ideal society every member is responsible for some definite, particular task.

—London Convention Address.

September 24

It has been proved by careful, scientific experiment that a wine-glass of liquor will increase the action of the heart so as to cause it to do every twenty-four hours from an eighth to a quarter more work than is necessary in driving the blood throughout the system, thus weakening and wearing out the system with every heart-beat.

—Danger Signals.

September 25

There is nothing so good for a young man as to have a home of his own and a pretty wife to pour out his tea on the other side of the cosey supper-table if he gets the right girl to preside over his tea-table, but not otherwise.

—The Mossback Correspondence.

September 26

The Society of Christian Endeavor was born of a revival, and was the outcome of a real, felt necessity, the necessity of training and guiding aright the young Christians who might otherwise stray away.

—WAYS AND MEANS.

September 27

The children and youth must breathe for themselves the pure air of religious truth; they must eat for themselves of the Living Bread; * * * they must exercise themselves frequently and constantly in the performance of every religious duty which is appropriate to their years and attainments. Thus only will they become "strong in the Lord and in the power of his might."

—AIDS TO ENDEAVOR.

September 28

Instruction—wise, patient, careful instruction—is most important for the growth of the young soul in the way of eternal life; but constant effort on his own part to make known the love of Jesus is no less important.

—AIDS TO ENDEAVOR.

September 29

We think that the contribution-box is passed pretty often, and that a large sum must be raised for the conversion of the heathen at home and abroad in the hundred thousand churches of our land; but for every dollar that goes into the missionary society two hundred dollars go into the till of the rumseller.

—DANGER SIGNALS.

September 30

To put the matter briefly, the duty of the prayer-meeting committee is to have a good prayer-meeting, and until it has succeeded in having this according to the number and ability of the society with which it is connected it has dismally failed of reaching its highest plane of service.

—THE CHRISTIAN ENDEAVOR MANUAL.

October 1

The vacation season is over. The annual rest-days are past days. We shall prove whether we have deserved our holiday by the way we plunge into our work.

—PLUNGE IN.

October 2

Let us have done with the old heresy that there is power in littleness. The Gideon's band story is entirely misapplied where it is made to teach that only a select few can be Gideons, or that a small army can fight God's battles better than a great one when the soldiers of the large army are equally devoted and obedient. All hail, then, to this "sound of a going in the tops of the mulberry-trees."

—The Opening Guns of the Fall Campaign.

October 3

Young Christians may make mistakes in working for Christ, but they make a greater mistake in not working for him. No failure in making the attempt is so bad as to fail to make it. Anything rather than spiritual death. Only let there be vigorous life, and guidance can readily be supplied.

—Training the Church of the Future.

October 4

It is worth quite as much to the Christian to know how to give as how to speak or pray in public.

—Ways and Means.

October 5

Follow back the history of almost any man or woman distinguished for good or evil, and you will find, if you could but know the truth, that at the door of life stands a mother of like nature and similar characteristics, sending the child forth with a blessing or a curse for mankind. But it is not simply the careers that fill the eye of history, and the names that spring to the lips of cheering crowds, whom the mothers have blessed or cursed.

—Looking Out on Life.

October 6

If you look straight in the speaker's eye, you will help him marvellously. If the sympathetic lines in your face and the play of the appreciative smile about your mouth tell him that you are following him, and catch his point, and believe in what he says, he will make a better address than he otherwise could.

—Convention Manners.

October 7

Let me earnestly appeal to you young people in your own lives to hold on to the idea of heroic service, to live "the difficult life." You

are retrograding and losing ground when you
find nothing hard to do for Christ, and
attempt no hard thing for him. If it has
become easy to you to say your verse in meeting, then do the difficult thing, and give your
personal testimony. If personal testimony is
easy, do the next difficult thing, and throw
yourself into the work of some committee that
takes time and strength and energy. The man
or woman who never does a difficult thing for
Christ's sake will just as surely become a
weakling with soft and flaccid spiritual muscles as the would-be athlete will become "soft"
who never takes any hard physical exercise.

The strenuous provisions of the Christian
Endeavor pledge are not matters of chance;
they did not happen to be incorporated. They
are part of God's plan for Christian Endeavor.
I do not care much for the form of words.
Change the form of the usually adopted pledge,
if you must, but keep one idea, the difficult
idea, the strenuous thought of doing what
Christ would have us do.

—The Difficult Life.

October 8

The chief office of every church and minister
of the gospel is to present the constructive,

building truths, to lift up the cross and the great Sufferer upon it as the only redemption of a lost race, to tell of the safe haven, and to point out the good roadstead where tempest-tossed vessels on life's ocean may ride out the storm; but it is also the duty of every church and preacher of the gospel to warn the mariner of approaching gales. The red flag saves life as well as the breakwater and the lighthouse.

—DANGER SIGNALS.

October 9

A man recently told me that he had lived all his life in London, but had never seen the Tower. There are many people in Buffalo who have never seen Niagara Falls, and tens of thousands in Boston who have never climbed Bunker Hill Monument. So there are millions of intelligent people in the world who have lived all their lives with this towering fact staring them in the face from every page of history, but have never seen it. There are multitudes in whose ears has been sounding as with cataract roar this tremendous truth spoken by the voice of God himself: "Obey my voice, and I will be your God, and ye shall be my people;" and yet they have never heard it.

—OLD LANTERNS FOR PRESENT PATHS.

October 10

Look back once in a while over the past, but do not be continually looking back or your head may get turned.

—THE MOSSBACK CORRESPONDENCE.

October 11

In this connection we see the efficacy of the milder virtues, meekness, gentleness, long-suffering, patience. They are great soul-growers. The strenuous politician has little use for them. The jingo laughs them to scorn. But the Saviour of mankind put them all in one chapter of blessedness, and left out of his beatitudes all the high-sounding martial qualities which the world is so fond of lauding. The one class of virtues grows character; the other, reputations; and he always puts the emphasis where it belongs.

—SOUL-GROWING AND SOUL-DWARFING.

October 12

There can be no beautiful, symmetrical unfolding of the new life without constant acknowledgment of Him who is that life.

—AIDS TO ENDEAVOR.

October 13

Worldly parents will have worldly children. The law of spiritual heredity is more certain than that of physical heredity. It is more certain that religiously indifferent parents will preside over religiously indifferent households than that blue-eyed fathers and mothers will have a blue-eyed flock of children.

—Training the Church of the Future.

October 14

You are serving your country best when you are serving God best.

—Old Lanterns for Present Paths.

October 15

Familiarity with the mere shell in which the Spirit has hidden the divine truth is of great worth. But the earnest young soul is not long content with the words of Scripture; he will soon want to know its hidden meaning; he will desire to get at the heart of the gospel. And so Bible-reading has led to Bible-study, and Bible-study often to a search for the deep things of God.

—Training the Church of the Future.

October 16

Occasionally the persistent hostility of the pastor, and far more often his indifference, kills or discourages a society, and makes it well-nigh impossible for it to do its best work. Many a society, I regret to say, has thus failed to reach its ideal, a failure for which the pastor is very largely, if not wholly, responsible. For such it seems to me the last day may have a serious hour of reckoning. A society with a sympathetic, earnest, and helpful pastor rarely, if ever, as has been said, fails to accomplish good results.

—THE CHRISTIAN ENDEAVOR MANUAL.

October 17

The religion of Christ is as germane to the heart of the boy or girl as to the heart of the father or mother. Why should not the lad speak of Jesus' love in his own way, as well as the father in his way? The ten or twelve-year-old boy will not talk at a meeting or anywhere else like the sixty-year-old deacon, but he can talk in his own way about Christ in the prayer-meeting as he talks in his own way about bats and balls on the playground, or about his lessons at the breakfast-table.

—YOUNG PEOPLE'S PRAYER-MEETINGS.

October 18

I thank God that there are so many wise and devout mothers in this world of ours, so few, comparatively, that are careless and godless and prayerless. How few there are who do not bring the little hands together at night, and teach the little lips to say "Our Father"! The brightest spot in the future outlook for America and the world is right here, that the race of pious mothers is not dying out.

—Looking Out on Life.

October 19

It is well to be influenced by the experience of others, and to adopt and adapt their wise and successful plans; for to heed and to practise them is often only another way of listening to God's voice speaking through them.

—What Shall We Do?

October 20

One test of a truth is that it is universal. Faith is faith in India and Kamchatka. Hope is hope in the New World and the Old. Charity is the "greatest of these" at the equator and the pole. So it is in all lesser matters that have in them the elements of universal truth. Here is the test of the value of an idea, of a movement, of an organization. Is it a temporary expedient that meets some local temporary need, or is it a satisfaction for a universal need? Is it a post to which something may be tied for a little, or is it a tree, with deep-running roots and wide-arching branches, which grows with the years, and whose seed takes root in any fertile soil? Thus can movements be tested.

—Training the Church of the Future.

October 21

A prayerful leader is the one whom the Holy Spirit honors and uses.

—Aids to Endeavor.

October 22

The prayer-meeting is sometimes called the thermometer of the church. It is this, but it is a good deal more; it registers the spiritual warmth of the church, to be sure; but it also generates this warmth. You can tell not only what the life of the church is, but largely what it will be for the future, from the vigor and interest of the prayer-meeting.

—The Christian Endeavor Manual.

October 23

As the baby must kick its feet and wave its ineffectual arms if it is well and strong; as the boy and girl must romp and play, and exercise their muscles, whether a gymnasium is provided for them or not; so there seems to be something in the nature of the young Christian that demands exercise. He must do something for himself. He will be stifled and dwarfed if everything is done for him.

—TRAINING THE CHURCH OF THE FUTURE.

October 24

To confess Christ does not imply the ability to make a good speech; it does not require training in rhetoric and elocution; it simply means the expression of love, which is as natural and appropriate for the young soul as for the flower to bloom or the bird to fly. But even the bird must have room to fly; the caged canary does not gain strength of wing. The plant must have a plot of ground and careful nurture before it opens its petals. So we believe that special provision should be made for every young Christian that he may not settle back into the ranks of the dumb and lifeless, who have mouths, but speak not.

—YOUNG PEOPLE'S PRAYER-MEETINGS.

October 25

The influence of nineteen hours in the best home on earth can be counteracted by five hours at school. The carefully nurtured boy, who for a dozen years has been kept from contamination in the home, may have a foul seed planted in his heart by a half-hour's contact with the rotten life of an unclean boy to whom he looks up as his elder and superior. The careful training of years may be undone, in a measure, at least, by an evil book or picture, or by a persistent sneer at religious things. So there is need of buttressing the best home on earth with other influences which shall help to mould the character for God.

—TRAINING THE CHURCH OF THE FUTURE.

October 26

In fact, the history of the evangelical church for the last hundred years is very largely the history of the prayer-meeting. Where this meeting has commanded the respect and the attention and the devotion of the members, the church has flourished; where it has declined and enlisted only the languid interest of a small fraction of the church-members, the whole life of the church has suffered in consequence.

—THE CHRISTIAN ENDEAVOR MANUAL.

October 27

To sin is to turn the back, to repent is to turn the face, to God. So simple and yet so radical is the great truth of salvation.

—OLD LANTERNS FOR PRESENT PATHS.

October 28

A lie that is easy to start may be impossible to refute. Every man owes it not only to his neighbor, but to himself, either to utterly disregard the scandalous rumor or to follow it up and prove its falsity or truth. Do not be deceived by the strength and breadth of its wing; see if it has legs and can stand.

—THE MOSSBACK CORRESPONDENCE.

October 29

As I write these words on the train, the porter is lighting the Pintsch lights in the lamps over my head. There are four burners in each lamp; but he touches the match to only one of them, and, when that blazes, the others then catch fire from it; and in a second all are alight. So it is with you. Light your own torch, and others will catch fire from it.

—WHAT IS A REVIVAL?

October 30

Are you dazzled by the lives of generals, Senators, millionaires, or great men of letters? Consider the cross ere looking at the crown. It is a grand thing to win the crown. Try for it. Try with all the manhood there is in you. You are worth little if you do not make the trial. Let no word of mine discourage you. But try no short cuts. Count the cost, and then do valiant battle. Determine to win all these good things, but win them legitimately.

—DANGER SIGNALS.

October 31

When Henry Wilson, who was vice-president of the United States on the same ticket with Gen. Grant, was converted in mature life, prominent politician and statesman though he was, he went around among his companions and friends in Natick, many of them old and hardened men, urging them to come to the revival meetings, and to go forward for prayers; and as a result many came into the Kingdom with him. How many will you bring with you this winter? The next few weeks will answer this question.

—THESE COMING WEEKS, WHAT WILL THEY BRING?

November 1

The bloom on the peach, once brushed off, does not return. Paint it ever so skilfully, you cannot restore its bloom. The virgin lily, once crumpled and bruised, is never itself again, however you press out its white petals. The snow, smirched and blackened, is never again the symbol of purity that it was when it fell from heaven. Therefore I would say to you with words burning hot if I could compass them, Beware, beware, beware of the first step on the road that may lead you at last to the pillory, to take your place beside the outcast woman with the blazing scarlet letter on her breast.

—Looking Out on Life.

November 2

The "because" is always followed by the "therefore."

—Old Lanterns for Present Paths.

Alas! alas for the young man who will not learn by the awful experience of the bleeding myriads who have been hacked and slaughtered by strong drink or licentiousness!

—The Mossback Correspondence.

November 3

Nothing can ever take the place of home training. At the best, other methods can only supplement and round out the nurture of the home, or can make up in some little measure for the defects or lack of home training. The mother's knee, the father's kindly care, form the very best possible means for the Christian nurture of children.

—TRAINING THE CHURCH OF THE FUTURE.

November 4

Let us not vote for any candidate unless on careful and prayerful thought we believe his triumph will be for the welfare of the land. Break with the past if need be. Break with your party if you must, but never break with your conscience.

—CONCERNING THE BURNING QUESTION OF THE DAY.

November 5

We need to get over the impression so widely prevalent that the soul of a grown person is a little more valuable than the soul of a child, and that it is a greater triumph to win such a soul for the Kingdom.

—TRAINING THE CHURCH OF THE FUTURE.

November 6

Plunge into life's duties, young man. Don't be always preparing for them and never getting at them.

—PLUNGE IN.

November 7

Search history through, and tell me whether you can find a single instance in nation or family where godlessness, debauchery, and disobedience of the laws of God brought permanent peace and prosperity. Unhesitatingly I dare to challenge the strictest, most careful research where the history of nation or family can be seen as a whole.

—OLD LANTERNS FOR PRESENT PATHS.

November 8

The reason why the false or defective faiths of Buddha and Mohammed and of the Greek and the Latin churches have so tremendous a hold on the life of the world to-day is that their adherents are never ashamed to declare their allegiance to their religion. Five times a day the devout Turk will pray with his face towards Mecca. The Buddhist will mutter half the day, "I believe in Buddha; I believe in

Buddha." The humblest Russian peasant will bless his black crust before all his fellows as he begins his humble meal. The English-speaking evangelical Christian, of all men, seems to be the most shamefaced concerning his religion, and this reluctance to acknowledge one's faith accounts in no small measure for the small influence which the purest faith in the world exercises upon the outside public.

—THE CHRISTIAN ENDEAVOR MANUAL.

November 9

I believe the great danger in these days is not of asking people too often to decide for Christ, or of asking it in an unwise, perfunctory, or unpleasant way, but of not giving the invitation at all.

—DRAWING THE NET.

November 10

The minister who is too busy or too preoccupied to care for the young is too busy to build up his church. The true servant of God will find the time and make the opportunity. He will adapt himself to this work, however few were his gifts in this direction originally. He will gain for himself the young heart that he may win the young, so that at the last, when his account is demanded, he may say, "Here am I, Lord, and the children whom thou hast given me."

—Training the Church of the Future.

November 11

Thank God that the gospel is not losing its power upon the lives of mankind!

—Advance Steps at Cincinnati, 1901.

November 12

How many of our young men are drifting about from place to place, looking for the easy spot; dissatisfied with this because the work is hard, and with that because the hours are long, and with the other place because the pay is small; unwilling to do their honest best because of some fancied grievance of work or pay; unwilling to do a stroke of work that they can live without doing, always waiting, like Mr. Micawber, for something to turn up, that shall furnish a snug berth and demand no equivalent of muscle or skill or brain! That is the gambler's spirit, whether you ever risked a cent or handled a cue in your life.

—Danger Signals.

November 13

You cannot wash your heart as you can your pocket-handkerchief. To keep your heart clean is comparatively easy; to cleanse it when once it is befouled, is an Augean task.

—Looking Out on Life.

November 14

To know God! Ah! this is knowledge indeed. It brings wisdom beyond any university course, beyond anything that travel or genius can give; and it is within the reach of every poorest and least-gifted stay-at-home.

To become acquainted with God! That means the best society. Emperors and nobles can have no such society as the humblest child of God, unless they, too, acquaint themselves with him.

—Spiritual Acquaintance.

November 15

There is no better thermometer to the real spiritual life of a church than its young people's work.

—Training the Church of the Future.

November 16

"Let the redeemed of the Lord say so," is an exhortation of the Psalmist which was never more needed than to-day. A sure precursor of a revival, as some one has said, would be to find all the members of the church of one mind and in one place and all acknowledging their love and devotion to the Lord. This was the Pentecostal sign of the great revival in which the church began, and it would be no less indicative of an awakening that would arouse the world to the claims of Christ to-day.

—THE CHRISTIAN ENDEAVOR MANUAL.

November 17

For various reasons our churches have come to contain many silent partners, many names of those who do not serve. Social considerations, decline of early zeal, physical incapacity, have filled our church-rolls, and have not multiplied our church-workers. I am not finding fault or indulging in a cheap fling at the laziness of Christians. I am stating a fact. Some counteracting forces were needed. Here is one of them, a society whose ideal, like Wesley's is, "At it, and all at it, and always at it"; a society that finds a task for the least as well as the greatest, for the youngest and most diffident as well as for the few natural-born leaders.

—THE CHRISTIAN ENDEAVOR MANUAL.

November 18

A community is not divided against itself when some members cultivate the soil, and others work in the shop, and others go to buying and selling, and still others become lawyers and doctors. Away with the mediæval notion that all members of the church must necessarily be doing the same things at the same time and in the same way, if the unity of the church is to be preserved!

—WHAT THE Y. M. C. A. HAS DONE FOR THE CHURCH.

November 19

I believe family life is the one great pervasive influence, next to the religion of Christ, that keeps society sweet and politics comparatively pure, and saves the nation from the degeneracy and corruption of Babylon and Egypt, Greece and Rome.

—BRITISH AND AMERICAN HOME LIFE.

November 20

The process of conversion may be a very gentle and simple one. The child may never know the exact moment of the turn in his pathway. But sometime the turn was made, sometime he made the choice; and, though there was no wrench of old habits, no upheaval of the old nature, no earthquake shock or tornado of passion, his whole future life, if he has indeed entered into the Kingdom, proves that there was a choice that placed him among the children of God.

—TRAINING THE CHURCH OF THE FUTURE.

November 21

The church or the charity which cannot live without grab-bags and guess-cakes had a thousand times better die.

—DANGER SIGNALS.

November 22

It would be amusing, were it not so sad, to observe the ingenuity of the devil in offering our young people a ride on one of the little silver horses of chance. Here is that noble institution, the church fair. Of course it is all right, the boy or girl thinks, to attend a church fair, and here in the fair is a guess-cake, or a grab-bag, or Pandora's box, or Fortune's well, or some chance to invest a dime or a quarter, with the chance of drawing an unknown prize. If there is anything to be reprobated or despised, it is just this species of gambling.

—DANGER SIGNALS.

November 23

Within the banks of faith and joy, of constant service and unselfish devotion, our lives may move with ever-increasing momentum and power until at last the ocean of our desires is reached, and we lose the stream of our life only to find it in the ocean of God.

—THE RHINE OF LIFE.

November 24

God has permitted evil in the world, but he has compelled it for the most part to hide its head. It goes abroad in the night, not in the daytime. It recruits its forces in dark cellars. It has its hiding-place in the outlaw's cave, where the light of the sun never pierces, and, if we cannot extirpate it, we should not parade it in the brightness of day. One great demoralizer of our times is this parade of evil.

—DANGER SIGNALS.

November 25

The great blessings of the past year have been spiritual blessings, not the turkeys, or the apples, or the dollars that have fallen to our lot; and these gifts should be repaid in kind, passed on as they are received.

—PRACTICAL THANKSLIVING FOR ENDEAVORERS.

November 26

Our neighbor, too, has his place in every true Thanksgiving Day. If we gorge ourselves with the good things God has given us, with never a thought of the friendless and the poor, we take our place with the swine at the trough, and deserve about as little consideration of God or man.

—A PROGRAMME FOR THANKSGIVING DAY.

November 27

In every life there are times of strain and stress and up-stream tug. The current is against us. Circumstances are adverse. Passions are impetuous. The stream of events, which we cannot control, is setting down-stream, while we are bound up. All we can do for a time is to struggle. We seem to make no headway. At the end of the day, the week, the year, we seem to be very near our starting-point. Nevertheless, our prow is always pointing up-stream, and that is much. We have not weakly yielded to circumstances, and that is more. We have not allowed ourselves to drift, and that in a young man's life is almost everything.

Courage! There is smoother water ahead! At any rate, it is quite as necessary to go up as down, if it is slower work. Our progress is not measured by the distance we gain, but by the struggle.

God knows the power of the current against us, as the engineer knows the force of the Rhine. He expects of us what we can do, and nothing more.

—THE RHINE OF LIFE.

November 28

The earth is a big, iron-ribbed craft sailing through space at an incredible rate. We are passengers all. But the Captain is on the bridge. He is responsible. His sleepless eye in fog and storm guides our course.

We have but our daily duty and daily play to do, just as well as we can, trusting to him the future, which we cannot foresee or alter. There is no other divine sedative like this, no other anti-worry medicine.

—A Midwinter Hurricane in Mid-Ocean.

November 29

As I write these words, I am speeding toward Liverpool to take the steamer for home. You who have not been absent for nine months, journeying in many lands, among Chinese Boxers, on Siberian rivers, stuck on mud-banks, waiting days in the wilderness with a burned bridge between you and all you love best, cannot realize what that word "home" means.

There is another sentiment, homely and uninspired, but none the less true, to which we can also subscribe:—

> "East, west,
> Hame's best."

—On Seas and Shores.

November 30

It is my great desire to glorify the routine of my life, to ennoble all its homely, every-day, unexciting tasks. I know of one way to do this, and only one, I must begin the day aright. The Quiet Hour with God is the great ennobler of little duties. It gilds with its own radiance every humdrum task. Then I want to carry the spirit of the Quiet Hour into every smallest action of the day. I want to take it to the breakfast-table with me, and down the hill to the railway station, and into the city on the cars, and up the elevator to my office, and to have the abiding Presence there all the day. In this spirit I wish to write every letter, and see every caller, and answer every request, and endure every unforeseen interruption which often breaks the day into seemingly useless fragments. I invite you, dear friends, to join me in this effort to irradiate humdrum, commonplace, every-day tasks with light from the other world.

—At the Old Desk Again.

December 1

We may sometimes have some questioning as to whether He will give us in response to our prayers wealth, or health, or influence, or power; for all these may be asked for selfishly, and may harm rather than bless us.

But, when we ask for spiritual gifts, and ask these, not for ourselves alone, but for young people the world around, can we doubt that His promise is ours, "If ye then, being evil, know how to give good gifts unto your children, how much more shall your heavenly Father give the Holy Spirit to them that ask Him?"

—December the First, Nineteen Hundred and Three.

December 2

All honor to the men who struggle on, and drag their obstacles with them, not whining or croaking or demanding sympathy, but just struggling on and up in spite of everything. Verily they will have their reward.

—The Rhine of Life.

December 3

The society was not made for its committees, but the committees are made for the society, that it might be a working organization.

—The Christian Endeavor Manual

December 4

I look upon it as one of the first duties of a child of God to tell the glad news to others. "Let the redeemed of the Lord say so."

—A New Zealand Address.

December 5

Our lives are very much as are our early dreams of life. If we start with noble ideals, the lives will pretty certainly be noble. If the ideals are degraded, the lives will pretty certainly be degraded.

—Danger Signals.

December 6

I believe in God's leading, not because I have read about it in history, and heard others talk about it; not simply because I believe the Bible, but because I have often experienced it in my own life. He has guarded me from untold evil when, as I afterward found, I was upon its brink.

He has kept me from doing the thing which I most wanted to do, because my way, as I now see, would have been disastrous. He has sent sickness and suffering when, as I now see, they were much better for me than health and happiness would have been.

—God's Leading in Our Lives.

December 7

Dirt and trash go together in literature as well as in the scavenger's cart. The dirty is always trashy; the trashy is usually dirty.

—Danger Signals.

December 8

One word that our Lord Jesus came to earth especially to emphasize is the word "Father." As applied to God it was almost unknown before he came. Heathen religions were ignorant of it, and even the Old Testament knows comparatively little of God as the Father of his people. He is the Shepherd, the Shield, the Sun, the High Tower, the Rock of our defence; and a hundred other names are his in the psalms and the prophets; but it was for Christ to reveal and emphasize the new and more blessed name, "Our Father."

On a railway journey I have just read through the Gospel of Matthew with this in view, to find how often Christ uses the word "Father" when speaking of God or to him, and I find that no less than thirty-six times in this one Gospel is this word used.

—CHILDREN OF GOD.

December 9

There is a danger in routine and humdrum as well as a blessing; and if, never looking up and out, we look into the ever-deepening rut, it will become a ditch, and our last ditch at that.

—AT THE OLD DESK AGAIN.

December 10

Better let the mind be empty than fill it with seeds which will inevitably produce an abundant crop of disease and death.

—Danger Signals.

December 11

How lavishly God bestows his gifts! An artist spends half a year in painting a single picture of the snow, three feet wide; and then it is often a poor, unreal, imperfect thing. God every morning covers all Scandinavia with a new snow picture, and on this gigantic canvas every minutest detail of leaf and twig and tender tree stem is as perfect as if it was the only one he had ever painted. During the day perhaps the sun wipes out the picture, but the next morning he paints it all over again, and repeats the picture perhaps a hundred times during the winter.

—In Snowland.

December 12

You can make it your business to live and proclaim the gospel while you serve behind a counter, or on a railway-train, or on a policeman's beat, "to pay expenses."

—Told at Midnight in a Sleeping-Car.

December 13

Many revivals can be traced, so far as human agency goes, directly to the prayer of some individual Christian, often a humble, inconspicuous Christian; sometimes to the prayer of a helpless invalid, who could never attend a prayer-meeting.

What God has done, God will do, if we are ready for him to work through us. Why may not the coming revival begin in your heart?

—A CALL TO PRAYER FOR A GREAT AWAKENING.

December 14

Smut always crocks. Pitch always sticks. When soot is in the air, it is just as likely to fall on your head as anywhere else; and the smut of these dirty periodicals is actually in the air to-day. Every age has its peculiar dangers, and needs its peculiar, trumpet-toned warnings. One note of alarm which we need to sound to-day, in this latter part of the nine-teenth century, is, "Beware of vile books."

—DANGER SIGNALS.

December 15

What we give is a test of what we are.

—"THIS GRACE ALSO."

December 16

"Holiday" is very near akin to "holy day." Its root and origin are the same. While we are enjoying the holidays, let us not forget the holy days that are coming, or fail to make the most of them when they come.

—HOLIDAYS AND HOLY DAYS.

December 17

If we remember our Latin derivations aright, "inculcate" means to grind in as with the heel, or literally "to heel in." "Educate" means to draw out. We need to educate the religious nature of the child as well as to inculcate the truth. This "drawing out" is more difficult than the "heeling in," but it is also more important.

—THE TRAINING OF YOUNG CHRISTIANS.

December 18

One day of crisis in my life, as so many others could say if they were relating their own story, was the day when I made up my mind, not only to be Christ's, but to let others know it. I remember well the little old-fashioned chapel of the country church, with its hard, straight-backed seats. I can remember now where I sat, though I was then scarcely thirteen years of age; and, if I should tell you the whole truth, I should have to confess that it was more than thirty years ago. I had no remarkable experience, no blinding light from heaven, no impulse that I could not resist if I had chosen to resist it; but I did know my duty, and I determined, as a million boys have done before and since, to try to do it; and, when the minister that had charge of that prayer-meeting, who was also my dear father, asked the question that so many ministers before and since have asked, whether there were any who were willing to acknowledge their love for Christ for the first time, I stood up, quite alone, if I remember rightly. I do not think I said a word, but that one act before all the people who were present committed me to the side of Christ.

—Matters of Personal Experience.

December 19

Meditation shows us that God is the source of supply for all our needs. "My soul thirsteth for God, for the living God."

Prayer digs a channel straight and true to this source of supply. "Ask, and ye shall receive."

Devotional reading of the word of God keeps the channel from becoming clogged with selfishness and self-seeking. It keeps us from simply teasing God for material blessings and nothing more. "My God shall supply all your need."

—THE FERTILE FIELD OF THE DESERT.

December 20

Almost all phrases that have become stereotyped by use, and even savor of cant because of vain repetition, have a deep reason for being. * * * Whenever you meet a word or phrase discarded or allowed to fall into "innocuous desuetude" because it is supposed to be meaningless cant, it is well to examine it carefully. It is probably an expressive gem of the first water. It is more than likely to be a diamond dulled by familiarity and thoughtless use.

—THE WILDCAT'S CHRISTMAS LESSON.

December 21

It is as natural for the young Christian to talk about his Saviour as for him to talk about his father, whom he loves next to his Saviour; and all training which intentionally

or unintentionally leads him to shut up the
love for either in his heart, without giving
utterance to it, is false and pernicious.
Instruction—wise, patient, careful instruction—is most important for the growth of
the young soul in the way of eternal life;
but constant effort on his own part to make
known the love of Jesus is no less important.
There can be no beautiful, symmetrical
unfolding of the new life without constant
acknowledgment of Him who is that life.

—Young People's Prayer-Meetings.

December 22

The other day, in a Christian Endeavor
meeting in Paris, the testimony that touched
my heart the most was that of a young lady,
who told us how, when she first spoke for her
Master in an Endeavor meeting, hesitating
and trembling and afraid of her own voice, as
she sat down, a little girl by her side, who
knew of her bashfulness, reached over and
took her hand with a comforting squeeze.
She said no word, but that gesture told of the
little girl's love and sympathy. It was one of
the steps that unconsciously led two souls up
the table-lands and into the sunlight of God's
presence.

But what is our whole system of Christian Endeavor if it is not a series of unconscious steps up invisible mountains? The prayer-meetings, in a sense, are routine affairs; fulfilling the pledge, in our discouraged moments, may seem like a perfunctory obligation; the committees, like the lifeless parts of a machine; but one great object of the Society is to form habits of well-doing, habits of confession, of devotion, of service.

—CONCERNING MORAL MOUNTAIN-CLIMBING.

December 23

Our pledge in its essence is not only the covenant of the Bible; it is the pledge of the Covenanters of Scotland, of the Pilgrims of New England, of the Huguenots of France, of the Waldenses, of the Lollards. Our pledge is the covenant of every Christian church adapted to young people of all churches. It is the spoken or unspoken vow of every soul that accepts Christ as Saviour. In its essence it is essential to the beginning of the Christian life.

Surely, then, Christian Endeavorers are right in putting such emphasis on their covenant pledge. It is, indeed, our Magna Charta. It has been approved by God, speak-

ing through the Bible and through history.
It is necessary because it is reasonable and
scriptural.

—CHRISTIAN ENDEAVOR IN THE NEW TESTAMENT.

December 24

Keep Christmas Day with your heart, and
not only with the fir-tree and the candle. Let
us hang the garlands within, and not all in
the windows that face upon the street.

—CHRISTMAS WITHOUT PLUM-PUDDING.

December 25

The Christmas idea is the gift idea. We
cannot separate the two ideas if we would, and
we would not if we could. The very mention
of the word "Christmas" reminds us of the
"unspeakable gift," and every poor little present that we make to one another reminds us
again of Him who was given to us in Beth-
lehem's manger on Christmas morn.

—A CHRISTMAS LETTER.

December 26

A great deal more depends upon what we
deem dull, commonplace, and prosaic than
upon the occasional lofty mountains of

achievement. In fact, I doubt whether in the moral world there are any startling Alpine heights to be climbed in a single journey.

Our daily ascent is more like our journey across the Nebraska prairies and the Colorado plains from the Missouri River to the Rocky Mountains. We are going uphill all the way, but so gradually that we do not know it until at last we stand five thousand feet above the sea, under the very shadow of Pike's Peak itself.

So every duty done, every act of kindness rendered, takes us one step up the hill, an inappreciable step, perhaps; a monotonous, weary sort of a step oftentimes, but yet a step that leads to real heights of moral grandeur.

—Concerning Moral Mountain-Climbing.

December 27

Teach the children at home, from the pulpit, and in the Sunday-school, that, if they can go to but one service, the preaching-service, where God is worshipped in the great congregation, is the place for them; and do everything, by making the church interesting and attractive to them, to lead them to feel that it is their service.

—Young People's Prayer-Meetings.

December 28

But in some way, dear friends, shall we not so pray and labor that the angels' song, as the months and years pass on, may mean more than it does now to thousands of our associate members, "Glory to God in the highest, on earth peace, good will to men"? God grant it!

—WAYS AND MEANS.

———

Frequent confession of Christ is not only a bulwark against worldliness and thoughtlessness, but a positive means of growth in grace.

* * * * * * * * *

The ability and willingness to express one's convictions are almost as vital to the Christian life as the possession of convictions. In fact, one can scarcely be said to have mastered that which he cannot or will not tell to another.

—TRAINING YOUNG CONVERTS.

———

December 29

You and I probably cannot become rich next year, however hard we work. We cannot become famous, even if we should sell ourselves body and soul to fame; but we may become God-like. There is absolutely no barrier in the way to this. The walls of a sick-room, the barbed-wire fence of our daily routine tasks, which seem so hard to overstep, the constraints of uncongenial associates, the bars of a prison, even—none of these can keep us from God or from becoming God-like.

—SOME CERTAIN POSSIBILITIES FOR NEXT YEAR.

December 30

I believe most heartily in New Year's resolutions; yes, in New Year's *pledges*. It is no real objection that they sometimes get frayed at the edge, cracked, or even broken. To say that we do not always live up to our best resolves is simply saying that we live in an imperfect world, and that we have "evil hearts of unbelief"; but we shall certainly live nearer to the standard of these resolutions than if we never made them.

—A FAMILIAR LETTER.

December 31

This is the last day of the year. We must leave it all behind us very soon. Let us leave other things behind us as well as the old year.

All hopelessness, all old ruts that are not good routes, all indifference to the best kind of Christian Endeavor work.

—FROM THE STEAMER'S DECK.

My good-by message to Christian Endeavorers is, Pray more; love more; give more; do more; be more.

—A FAMILIAR LETTER.

No, not farewell; that is not the best Christian word, but good-by, or, in other words, "God be with you," till we meet again.

—A FAMILIAR LETTER.

Some Popular Books

Daily Message for Christian Endeavorers, A.

By MRS. FRANCIS E. CLARK. Introduction by DR. CLARK.

373 pp., cloth, gilt top, illuminated cover-design, 12 full-page illustrations.
Boxed, $1.00.

This is a book for the Quiet Hour, the Prayer Meeting, and the Birthday. It is three books in one. There is a page for every day in the year, filled with the choicest thoughts of the best writers. The collection is the result of years of careful reading. A new feature in books of this kind is the place for birthday entries, space being given under every day in the year.

Morning Watch, The.

A BOOK FOR THE QUIET HOUR. By BELLE M. BRAIN.

414 pp., cloth, illustrated, gilt top. Boxed, $1.00.

366 gems, each a page in length, from the heart and brain and hand of the saints of God in all ages. A book of daily readings, giving a month with an author. This is one of the most interesting books of daily readings that has ever been compiled, as the authors speak from the hours of their richest and deepest experience.

Lincoln at Work.

By WILLIAM O. STODDARD.

Illustrations by SEARS GALLAGHER. Cloth, $1.00.

In a series of fascinating and most graphic chapters, Colonel Stoddard pictures the gaunt, ungainly politician, his rapid and marvellous rise to power, and that strange life in the White House, so appealing in its pathos, its quaint humor, and the profound tragedy that lay underneath it all. Many anecdotes are told, throwing a flood of light upon the times and the man.

From Life to Life.

By REV. J. WILBUR CHAPMAN, D.D.

Illuminated cover-design, cloth, $1.00.

Those who have ever heard Dr. Chapman speak have been impressed with the large number of anecdotes, incidents, stories, poems, etc., he has used in illustrating his talks. This illustrative material, gathered from many sources and touching many topics, will prove of great interest and value for personal reading, as well as an aid in reaching others.

How to Work—How to Play—How to Study.

By AMOS R. WELLS.

Three books uniformly bound in cloth; 75 cents each.
The three volumes, $2.00.

Three books on very practical subjects. This is a working nation, and yet few among its millions of workers know how to work to the best advantage. "Puttering," "Putting Off," "Taking Hints," "'Can' Conquers," "The Bulldog Grip," are specimen titles of the thirty-one chapters in "How to Work."

In "How to Play," the very first chapter is entitled "The Duty of Playing," which shows that the author believes in recreation. Practical chapters are given upon such themes as how to keep games fresh, inventing games, overdoing it, true recreation, etc.

In "How to Study," such topics as concentration of mind, night study, cramming, memory training, care of the body, are considered. Many illustrations and anecdotes are given, and the author makes full use of his experience as a teacher and college professor.

UNITED SOCIETY OF CHRISTIAN ENDEAVOR
BOSTON AND CHICAGO

TEMPLE SERIES

The Best Authors.
Copyrighted Books.
Superbly Bound in Cloth.
Illustrated.

THE books are beautifully bound, and stamped with original cover designs in colors and gold. Each volume contains an appropriate half-tone frontispiece. Too much cannot be said in praise of them. For gift purposes they cannot be excelled. 4 ¾ x 7 ¼ inches. Dainty cloth bindings. Illustrated.

Price, 35 cents each.

THE THREE WHYS. By Rev. Maltbie D. Babcock, D.D. Talks to young Christians.

THE FOUR G'S. By Rev. Theo. L. Cuyler, D.D. The Four G's are Grace, Grit, Growth, and Gratitude.

OLD LANTERNS FOR PRESENT PATHS. By Rev. F. E. Clark, D.D. Helpful thoughts from Jeremiah for young people.

JUST TO HELP. (Poems.) By Amos R. Wells. Poems appropriate to the title, written — just to help.

GOLDEN COUNSELS. By Dwight L. Moody. Practical subjects forcefully presented.

WELL BUILT. By Rev. Theodore L. Cuyler, D.D. Plain talks to young people.

HELPS UPWARD. By Rev. Wayland Hoyt, D.D. Apt illustrations of great themes.

A FENCE OF TRUST. By Mary F. Butts. Poems and Sonnets.

PLUCK AND PURPOSE. By William M. Thayer. Success, and how to obtain it.

LITTLE SERMONS FOR ONE. By Amos R. Wells. Heart-to-heart talks.

WISE LIVING. By Rev. George C. Lorimer, D.D. The gaining and wise use of money.

THE INDWELLING GOD. By Rev. Charles A. Dickinson, D.D. The power and purpose of a life of faith.

TACT. By Kate Sanborn. Racy essays on society's virtues and foibles.

YOUTH AND AGE. By Rev. James Stalker, D.D. A suggestive treatment of Ecclesiastes 12.

SUNSHINE. (Poems). By Mary D. Brine. Poems of cheer and encouragement.

MAKING THE MOST OF ONE'S SELF. By Rev. A. S. Gumbart, D.D. Practical talks to young men.

ANSWERED ! By Rev. J. Wilbur Chapman, D.D., Rev. R. A. Torrey, D.D., Rev. C. H. Yatman, Rev. Edgar E. Davidson, Thomas E. Murphy, and Rev. A. C. Dixon, D.D. Remarkable instances of answered prayer.

UNITED SOCIETY OF CHRISTIAN ENDEAVOR
BOSTON AND CHICAGO

QUIET HOUR BOOKS

CHAMBERS OF THE SOUL. By Rev. Cornelius Woelfkin, D.D. Cloth, 35 cents. The Quiet Hour Talks given by Dr. Woelfkin at the Cincinnati Christian Endeavor Convention, and which were enjoyed by so many thousands at that time.

DAY BY DAY. By Rev. J. Wilbur Chapman, D.D. Cloth, 35 cents. Thirty "meditations for the morning watch" — one for each day of the month.

DEEPER YET. By Rev. Clarence E. Eberman. Dainty cloth, 50 cents. A series of nearly thirty brief meditations, each based on some Scripture passage and excellently fitted for devotional use.

GOLDEN ALPHABET, THE. By Rev. Francis E. Clark, D.D. Cloth, 25 cents. Thirty-one choice selections from the works of Master John Tauler.

GREAT SECRET, THE. By Rev. Francis E. Clark, D.D. Dainty cloth binding, 30 cents. The secret of Health, Beauty, Happiness, Friend-making, Common Sense, and Success are all explained in "The Great Secret."

IMPROVEMENT OF PERFECTION, THE. By Rev. William E. Barton, D.D. Cloth, 35 cents. This is meant to help young Christians to a higher life by showing what kind of perfection God expects, and how it is to be gained.

INNER LIFE, THE. By Bishop John H. Vincent, D.D. Cloth, 35 cents; paper, 15 cents; two copies, 25 cents. "A study in Christian experience."

I PROMISE. By Rev. F. B. Meyer, B.A. Cloth, 35 cents. Its chapters deal with matters of the utmost importance to every Christian, whether he is an Endeavorer or not.

KINGDOM WITHIN, THE. By Rev. Francis E. Clark, D.D. Cloth, 25 cents. 31 choice selections from the "Imitation of Christ," by Thomas à Kempis.

LIVING AND LOVING. By Rev. Francis E. Clark, D.D. Cloth, 25 cents. 31 choice selections from the devotional works of Professor A. Tholuck.

MAN WHO SAID HE WOULD, THE. By Rev. J. Wilbur Chapman. Cloth, 35 cents. A most excellent book, with four Biblical characters as the subjects.

MY BEST FRIEND. By Rev. Floyd W. Tomkins. Cloth, 35 cents; paper, 15 cents; two copies, 25 cents. The six meditations for the Quiet Hour given by Dr. Tomkins at the Cincinnati Christian Endeavor Convention, entitled "Confessing Christ," "Trusting Christ," "Walking with Christ," "Serving Christ," "Nourished by Christ," and "Christ in Me."

PRESENCE OF GOD, THE. By Rev. Francis E. Clark, D.D. Cloth, 25 cents. 31 choice selections from the devotional works of Bishop Jeremy Taylor.

QUAINT THOUGHTS. By Belle M. Brain. Cloth, 25 cents. A delightful book made up from the writings of that famous old army chaplain, Thomas Fuller

SECRET OF A HAPPY DAY, THE. By Rev. J. Wilbur Chapman, D.D. Cloth, 50 cents; presentation edition, white cloth, gilt edge, 75 cents. The book is based upon the wonderful twenty-third psalm, which has brought joy and peace to so many sorrowing hearts.

SURRENDERED LIFE, THE. By Rev. J. Wilbur Chapman, D.D. Cloth, 35 cents; paper, 15 cents; two copies, 25 cents. The book sets forth the life "hid with Christ in God."

UNITED SOCIETY OF CHRISTIAN ENDEAVOR

BOSTON AND CHICAGO

www.ingramcontent.com/pod-product-compliance
Lightning Source LLC
Chambersburg PA
CBHW020948030426
42339CB00004B/7